DEREK WALCOTT
DREAM ON MONKEY MOUNTAIN

Derek Walcott was born in St. Lucia in 1930. His *Collected Poems: 1948–1984* was published in 1986, and his subsequent works include a book-length poem, *Omeros* (1990); a collection of verse, *The Bounty* (1997); and, in an edition illustrated with his own paintings, the long poem *Tiepolo's Hound* (2000). His most recent collections of plays are *The Haitian Trilogy* (2001) and *Walker and the Ghost Dance* (2002). He received the Nobel Prize in Literature in 1992.

ALSO BY DEREK WALCOTT

POEMS
Selected Poems
The Gulf
Another Life
Sea Grapes
The Star-Apple Kingdom
The Fortunate Traveller
Midsummer
Collected Poems: 1948–1984
The Arkansas Testament
Omeros
The Bounty
Tiepolo's Hound

PLAYS
Dream on Monkey Mountain and Other Plays
The Joker of Seville and O Babylon!
Remembrance and Pantomime
Three Plays: The Last Carnival; Beef, No Chicken;
  Branch of the Blue Nile
The Odyssey
The Haitian Trilogy
Walker and The Ghost Dance

ESSAYS
What the Twilight Says

DREAM ON MONKEY MOUNTAIN

Derek Walcott

Dream on Monkey Mountain
and *Other Plays*

FARRAR, STRAUS AND GIROUX
NEW YORK

FOR MY BROTHER, RODERICK,
ENGAGED AS LONG IN THE ONE ENDEAVOUR

Farrar, Straus and Giroux
19 Union Square West, New York 10003

Library of Congress catalog card number: 74-122827
ISBN: 0-374-508607

www.fsgbooks.com

29   28   27   26   25   24

Foreword

A playwright should let his work speak for itself, but in the ninth year of running a theatre company, and my nineteenth of writing plays in the West Indies, I began as a commemorative essay the lengthy prologue that follows. This essay should not be considered either as an apologia or a manifesto, something to pummel the reader's sympathy for the flaws in the plays. It merely tries to re-create the experience of a playwright with the company to which his plays became committed.

I cannot list all who have helped over the years but I must acknowledge my gratitude to the Rockefeller Foundation for a three-year grant; to Dr. John Harrison, Dr. Gerald Freund, Mr. John Gillespie, Mr. Henri Salvatori, Mr. George White, Mr. Dale Wasserman, Mr. Derek Knight, and Mr. Errol Barrow; and to my wife, Margaret, for sharing in all the irritating practicalities of play production.

D. W.

Trinidad
September 1970

Contents

DREAM ON MONKEY MOUNTAIN

I

But I see what it is, you are not from these parts, you don't know what our twilights can do. Shall I tell you?
Waiting for Godot

When dusk heightens, like amber on a stage set, those ramshackle hoardings of wood and rusting iron which circle our cities, a theatrical sorrow rises with it, for the glare, like the aura from an old-fashioned brass lamp is like a childhood signal to come home. Light in our cities keeps its pastoral rhythm, and the last home-going traffic seems to rush through darkness that comes from suburban swamp or forest in a noiseless rain. In true cities another life begins: neons stutter to their hysterical pitch, bars, restaurants and cinemas blaze with artifice, and Mammon takes over the switchboard, manipulator of cities; but here the light makes our strongest buildings tremble, its colour hints of rust, more stain than air. To set out for rehearsals in that quivering quarter-hour is to engage conclusions, not beginnings, for one walks past the gilded hallucinations of poverty with a corrupt resignation touched by details, as if the destitute, in their orange-tinted backyards, under their dusty trees, or climbing to their favelas, were all natural scene-designers and poverty were not a condition but an art. Deprivation is made lyrical, and twilight, with the patience of alchemy, almost transmutes despair into virtue. In the tropics noth-

3

ing is lovelier than the allotments of the poor, no theatre is as vivid, voluble and cheap.

Years ago, watching them, and suffering as you watched, you proffered silently the charity of a language which they could not speak, until your suffering, like the language, felt superior, estranged. The dusk was a raucous chaos of curses, gossip and laughter; everything performed in public, but the voice of the inner language was reflective and mannered, as far above its subjects as that sun which would never set until its twilight became a metaphor for the withdrawal of Empire and the beginning of our doubt.

Colonials, we began with this malarial enervation: that nothing could ever be built among these rotting shacks, barefooted backyards and moulting shingles; that being poor, we already had the theatre of our lives. So the self-inflicted role of martyr came naturally, the melodramatic belief that one was message-bearer for the millennium, that the inflamed ego was enacting their will. In that simple schizophrenic boyhood one could lead two lives: the interior life of poetry, the outward life of action and dialect. Yet the writers of my generation were natural assimilators. We knew the literature of Empires, Greek, Roman, British, through their essential classics; and both the patois of the street and the language of the classroom hid the elation of discovery. If there was nothing, there was everything to be made. With this prodigious ambition one began.

If, twenty years later, that vision has not been built, so that at every dusk one ignites a city in the mind above the same sad fences where the poor revolve, the theatre still an architectural fantasy, if there is still nothing around us, darkness still preserves the awe of self-enactment as the sect

4

gathers for its self-extinguishing, self-discovering rites. In that aboriginal darkness the first principles are still sacred, the grammar and movement of the body, the shock of the domesticated voice startling itself in a scream. Centuries of servitude have to be shucked; but there is no history, only the history of emotion. Pubescent ignorance comes into the light, a shy girl, eager to charm, and one's instinct is savage: to violate that ingenuousness, to degrade, to strip her of those values learnt from films and books because she too moves in her own hallucination: that of a fine and separate star, while her counterpart, the actor, sits watching, but he sits next to another hallucination, a doppelganger released from his environment and his race. Their simplicity is really ambition. Their gaze is filmed with hope of departure. The noblest are those who are trapped, who have accepted the twilight.

If I see these as heroes it is because they have kept the sacred urge of actors everywhere: to record the anguish of the race. To do this, they must return through a darkness whose terminus is amnesia. The darkness which yawns before them is terrifying. It is the journey back from man to ape. Every actor should make this journey to articulate his origins, but for these who have been called not men but mimics, the darkness must be total, and the cave should not contain a single man-made, mnemonic object. Its noises should be elemental, the roar of rain, ocean, wind, and fire. Their first sound should be like the last, the cry. The voice must grovel in search of itself, until gesture and sound fuse and the blaze of their flesh astonishes them. The children of slaves must sear their memory with a torch. The actor must break up his body and feed it as ruminatively as ancestral story-tellers fed twigs to the fire. Those who look from their darkness into the tribal fire must be bold enough to cross it.

The cult of nakedness in underground theatre, of tribal rock, of poverty, of rite, is not only nostalgia for innocence, but the enactment of remorse for the genocides of civilization, a search for the wellspring of tragic joy in ritual, a confession of aboriginal calamity, for their wars, their concentration camps, their millions of displaced souls have degraded and shucked the body as food for the machines. These self-soiling, penitential cults, the Theatre of the Absurd, the Theatre of Cruelty, the Poor Theatre, the Holy Theatre, the pseudo-barbarous revivals of primitive tragedy are not threats to civilization but acts of absolution, gropings for the outline of pure tragedy, rituals of washing in the first darkness. Their howls and flagellations are cries to that lost God which they have pronounced dead, for the God who is offered to slaves must be served dead, or He may change His chosen people.

The colonial begins with this knowledge, but it has taken one twenty years to accept it. When one began twenty years ago it was in the faith that one was creating not merely a play, but a theatre, and not merely a theatre, but its environment. Then the twilight most resembled dawn, then how simple it all seemed! We would walk, like new Adams, in a nourishing ignorance which would name plants and people with a child's belief that the world is its own age. We had no more than children need, and perhaps one has remained childish, because fragments of that promise still surprise us. Then, even the old rules were exciting! Imitation was pure belief. We, the actors and poets, would strut like new Adams in a nakedness where sets, costumes, dimmers, all the "dirty devices" of the theatre were unnecessary or inaccessible. Poverty seemed a gift to the imagination, necessity was truly a virtue, so we set our plays in the open, in natural, unphased light, and our subject was bare, "unaccommodated man." Today one writes this with more exhaustion than pride, for that innocence has been corrupted and society has taken the old direction. In these new nations art is a luxury, and the theatre the most superfluous of amenities.

Every state sees its image in those forms which have the mass appeal of sport, seasonal and amateurish. Stamped on that image is the old colonial grimace of the laughing nigger, steelbandsman, carnival masker, calypsonian and limbo dancer. These popular artists are trapped in the State's concept of the folk form, for they preserve the colonial demeanour and threaten nothing. The folk arts have become the symbol of a carefree, accommodating culture, an adjunct to tourism, since the State is impatient with anything which it cannot trade.

This is not what a generation envisaged twenty years ago, when a handful of childish visionaries foresaw a Republic devoted to the industry of art, for in those days we had nothing else. The theatre was about us, in the streets, at lampfall in the kitchen doorway, but nothing was solemnised into cultural significance. We recognised illiteracy for what it was, a defect, not the attribute it is now considered to be by revolutionaries. Language was earned, there was no self-contempt, no vision of revenge. Thus, for the young poet and actor, there was no other motivation but knowledge. The folk knew their deprivations and there were no frauds to sanctify them. If the old gods were dying in the mouths of the old, they died of their own volition. Today they are artificially resurrected by the anthropologist's tape-recorder and in the folk archives of departments of culture.

To believe in its folk forms the State would have to hallow not only its mythology but re-believe in dead gods, not as converts either, but as makers. But no one in the New World whose one God is advertised as dead can believe in innumerable gods of another life. Those gods would have to be an anthropomorphic variety of his will. Our poets and actors would have not only to describe possession but to enact it, otherwise we would have not art but blasphemy and blasphemy which has no fear is decoration. So now we are entering the "African" phase with our pathetic African carvings, poems and costumes, and our art objects are not sacred vessels placed on altars but goods placed on shelves for the tourist. The romantic darkness which they celebrate is thus another treachery, this time perpetrated by the intellectual. The result is not one's own thing but another minstrel show. When we produced Soyinka's masterpiece *The Road*, one truth, like the murderous headlamps of his mammy-wagons, transfixed us, and this was that our frenzy goes by another name, that it is this naming, ironically enough, which weakens our effort at being African. We tried, in the words of his Professor, to "hold the god captive," but for us, Afro-Christians, the naming of the god estranged him. Ogun was an exotic for us, not a force. We could pretend to enter his power but he would never possess us, for our invocations were not prayer but devices. The actor's approach could not be catatonic but rational; expository, not receptive. However, Ogun is not a contem-

8

plative but a vengeful force, a power to be purely obeyed. Like the Professor, only worse, we had lost both gods, and only blasphemy was left.

Since art is informed by something beyond its power, all we could successfully enact was a dance of doubt. The African revival is escape to another dignity, but one understands the glamour of its simplifications. Listen, one kind of writer, generally the entertainer, says: "I will write in the language of the people however gross or incomprehensible"; another says: "Nobody else go' understand this, you hear, so le' me write English"; while the third is dedicated to purifying the language of the tribe, and it is he who is jumped on by both sides for pretentiousness or playing white. He is the mulatto of style. The traitor. The assimilator. Yes. But one did not say to his Muse, "What kind of language is this that you've given me?" as no liberator asks history, "What kind of people is that that I'm meant to ennoble?", but one went about his father's business. Both fathers'. If the language was contemptible, so was the people. After one had survived the adolescence of prejudice there was nothing to justify. Once the New World black had tried to prove that he was as good as his master, when he should have proven not his equality but his difference. It was this distance that could command attention without pleading for respect. My generation had looked at life with black skins and blue eyes, but only our own painful, strenuous looking, the learning of looking, could find meaning in the life around us, only our own strenuous hearing, the hearing of our hearing, could make sense of the sounds we made. And without comparisons. Without any startling access of "self-respect." Yet, most of our literature loitered in the pathos of sociology, self-pitying and patronised. Our writers whined in the voices of twilight, "Look at this people! They may be degraded, but they are as good as you are. Look at what you have done to them." And their poems remained laments, their novels propaganda tracts, as if one general apology on behalf of the past would supplant imagination, would spare them the necessity of great art. Pastoralists of the African revival should know that what is needed is not new names for old things, or old names for old things, but the faith of using the old names anew, so that mongrel as I am, something prickles in me when I see the word Ashanti as with the word Warwickshire, both separately intimating my grandfathers' roots, both baptising this neither proud nor ashamed bastard, this hybrid, this West Indian. The power of the dew still shakes off of our dialects, which is what Césaire sings:

> Storm, I would say. River, I would command. Hurricane, I would say. I would utter "leaf." Tree. I would be drenched in all the rains, soaked in all the dews.

I I

Et c'est l'heure, O Poète, de décliner ton nom, ta naissance, et ta race . . .
St-John Perse: Exil

Yes. But we were all strangers here. The claim which we put forward now as Africans is not our inheritance, but a bequest, like that of other races, a bill for the condition of our arrival as slaves. Our own ancestors shared that complicity, and there is no one left on whom we can exact revenge. That is the laceration of our shame. Nor is the land automatically ours because we were made to work it. We have no more proprietorship as a race than have the indentured workers from Asia except the claim is wholly made. By all the races as one race, because the soil was stranger under our own feet than under those of our captors. Before us they knew the names of the forests and the changes of the sea, and theirs were the names we used. We began again, with the vigour of a curiosity that gave the old names life, that charged an old language, from the depth of suffering, with awe. To the writers of my generation, then, the word, and the ritual of the word in print, contained this awe, but the rage for revenge is hard to exorcise.

At nineteen, an elate, exuberant poet madly in love with English, but in the dialect-loud dusk of water-buckets and fish-sellers, conscious of the naked, voluble poverty around me, I felt a fear of that darkness which had swallowed up all fathers. Full of precocious rage, I was drawn, like a child's mind to fire, to the Manichean conflicts of Haiti's history. The parallels were there in my own island, but not the heroes: a black French island somnolent in its Catholicism and black magic, blind faith and blinder overbreeding, a society which triangulated itself mediaevally into land-baron, serf and cleric, with a vapid, high-brown bourgeoisie. The fire's shadows, magnified into myth, were those of the black Jacobins of Haiti.

They were Jacobean too because they flared from a mind drenched in Elizabethan literature out of the same darkness as Webster's Flamineo, from a flickering world of mutilation and heresy. They were moved by the muse of witchcraft, their self-disgust foreshadowed ours, that wrestling contradiction of being white in mind and black in body, as if the flesh were coal from which the spirit like tormented smoke writhed to escape. I repeat the raging metaphysics of a bewildered boy in this rhetoric. I can relive, without his understanding, a passion which I have betrayed. But they seemed to him, then, those slave-kings, Dessalines and Christophe, men who had structured their own despair. Their tragic bulk was massive as a citadel at twilight. They were our only noble ruins. He believed then that the moral of tragedy could only be Christian, that their fate was the debt exacted by the sin of pride, that they were punished by a white God as masters punished servants for presumption. He saw history as hierarchy and to him these heroes, despite their meteoric passages, were damned to the old darkness because they had challenged an ordered universe. He was in awe of their blasphemy, he rounded off their fate with the proper penitence, while during this discipleship which he served as devotedly as any embittered acolyte, the young Frantz Fanon and the already ripe and bitter Césaire were manufacturing the home-made bombs of their prose poems, their drafts for revolution, in the French-creole island of Martinique. They were blacker. They were poorer. Their anguish was tragic and I began to feel deprived of blackness and poverty. I had my own divisions too, but it was only later, when their prophecies became politics, that I was confronted with choice. My bitterness matched theirs but it concealed envy; my compassion was not less, but both were full of self-contempt and contained a yearning. Those first heroes of the Haitian Revolution, to me, their tragedy lay in their blackness. Yet one had more passion then, passion for reconciliation as well as change. It is no use repeating that this was not the way the world went, that the acolyte would have to defrock himself of that servitude. Now, one may see such heroes as squalid fascists who chained their own people, but they had size, mania, the fire of great heretics.

It is easy, twenty years later, to mock such ambition, to concede what a critic called its "fustian," yet the Jacobean style, its cynical, aristocratic flourish came naturally to this first play—the corruption of slaves into tyrants. Here were slaves who by divine right could never be kings, because by claiming kingship they abrogated the law of God. Despite my race, I could not believe that He would choose such people as his engines. Still, this tragedy's fiercest exchanges contained a self-frightening fury:

ARCHBISHOP
This is the curse of the nation,
Eating your own stomach, where the sickness is,
Your smell of blood offends the nostrils of God.

CHRISTOPHE
Perhaps the smell of sweat under my arms
offends that god too, quivering his white, crooked nostrils;
Well, tell him, after death, that it is honest
as the seven words of blood broken on his flesh, tell Him
the nigger smell that even kings must wear
is bread and wine to life.
I am proud, I have worked and grown
This country to its stature, tell Him that.

The theme has remained: one race's quarrel with another's God.

There was only one noble ruin in the archipelago: Christophe's massive citadel at La Ferrière. It was a monument to egomania, more than a strategic castle; an effort to reach God's height. It was the summit of the slave's emergence from bondage. Even if the slave had surrendered one Egyptian darkness for another, that darkness was his will, that structure an image of the inaccessible achieved. To put it plainer, it was something we could look up to. It was all we had.

I I I

I am thinking of a child's vow sworn in vain,
Never to leave that valley his fathers called their home.
                                                            Yeats

To be born on a small island, a colonial backwater, meant a precocious resignation to fate. The shoddy, gimcrack architecture of its one town, its doll-sized verandahs, jalousies and lacy eaves neatly perforated as those doilies which adorn the polished tables of the poor seemed so frail that the only credible life was nature. A nature without man, like the sea on which the sail of a canoe can seem an interruption. A nature with blistered aspects: grey, rotting shacks, the colour of the peasant woman's dress, which huddled on rocky rises outside the villages. But through nature one came to love the absence of philosophy, and, fatally, perhaps, the beauty of certain degradations.

In that innocent vagabondage one sought out the poor as an adventure, an illumination, only to arrive where, rooted like a rigid articulation of the rocks, the green and blue enamelled statue of the Virgin leaned from her niche, facing a green and blue Atlantic, like the peeling figurehead of a slave ship (in her various shrines her age could change from decorous matron to eager postulant), and where, back in the bleached, unpainted fishing village streets everyone seemed salted with a reek of despair, a life, a theatre, reduced to elementals. The acrid, shuttered smell of the poor was as potent and nocturnal as the odours of sex, with its intimacies of lowered Virgin lamps and coconutfibre mattresses until it seemed that a Catholic destitution was a state of grace which being part-white and Methodist I could never achieve. That life was measured as carefully as broken shop-bread by its rituals, it had dimpled the serene smile of Our Lady of the Rocks by its observance of five o'clock mass, rosaries, scapulars, coloured prints, lampions with perpetual flame floating in oil, vespers, fasts, feasts, and the shell-bordered cemeteries by the village river. The race was locked in its conviction of salvation like a freemasonry. There was more envy than hate towards it, and the love that stubbornly emerged showed like weeds through the ruined aisle of an abandoned church, and one worked hard for that love, against their love of priest and statue, against the pride of their resignation. One worked to have the "feel" of the island, bow, gunwhales and stern as jealously as the fisherman knew his boat, and, despite the intimacy of its size to be as free as a canoe out on the ocean.

That apprenticeship would mean nothing unless life were made so real that it stank, so close that you could catch the changes of morning and afternoon light on the rocks of the Three Sisters, pale brown rocks carious in the gargle of sea, could catch the flash of a banana leaf in sunlight, catch the smell of drizzled asphalt and the always surprisingly stale smell of the sea, the reek that chafes in the guts of canoes, and the reek of human rags that you once thought colorful, but, God give you that, in rage, a reek both fresh and resinous, all salted on the page, that dark catalogue of country-shop smells, the tang of raw, fine powdery cod, of old onions drying, of the pork-barrel, and the shelves of faded cloth, all folded round the fusty smell of the proprietor, some exact magical, frightening woman in tinted glasses, who emerged from the darkness like history.

There the materials began. They were given.

And the fishermen, those whom Jesus first drew to his net, they were the most blasphemous and bitter.

Theirs was a naked, pessimistic life, crusted with the dirty spume of beaches. They were a sect which had evolved its own signs, a vocation which excluded the stranger. The separation of town from countryside and countryside from sea challenged your safety, and all one's yearning was to enter that life without living it. It smelled strong and true. But what was its truth?

That in the "New Aegean" the race, of which these fishermen were the stoics, had grown a fatal adaptability. As black absorbs without reflection they had rooted themselves with a voracious, unreflecting calm. By all arguments they should have felt displaced, seeing this ocean as another Canaan, but that image was the hallucination of professional romantics, writer and politician. Instead, the New World Negro was disappointingly ordinary. He needed to be stirred into bitterness, thence perhaps to action, which means that he was as avaricious and as banal as those who had enslaved him. What would deliver him from servitude was the forging of a language that went beyond mimicry, a dialect which had the force of revelation as it invented names for things, one which finally settled on its own mode of inflection, and which began to create an oral culture of chants, jokes, folk-songs and fables; this, not merely the debt of history was his proper claim to the New World. For him metaphor was not a symbol but conversation, and because every poet begins with such ignorance, in the anguish that every noun will be freshly, resonantly named, because a new melodic inflection meant a new mode, there was no better beginning. It did not matter how rhetorical, how dramatically heightened the language was if its tone were true, whether its subject was the rise and fall of a Haitian king or a small-island fisherman, and the only way to re-create this language was to share in the torture of its articulation. This did not mean the jettisoning of "culture" but, by the writer's making creative use of his schizophrenia, an electric fusion of the old and the new.

So the people, like the actors, awaited a language. They confronted a variety of styles and masks, but because they were casual about commitment, ashamed of their speech, they were moved only by the tragi-comic and farcical. The tragi-comic was another form of self-contempt. They considered tragedy to be, like English, an attribute beyond them.

Clouds of heroes, young and old have died for me.
                    Gênet's Queen in "The Blacks"

The future of West Indian militancy lies in art. All revolutions begin amateurishly, with forged or stolen weapons,
but the West Indian artist knew the need for revolt without knowing what weapons to use, and just as a comfort-
able, self-hugging pathos hid in the most polemical of West
Indian novels, so there was in the sullen ambition of the
West Indian actor a fear that he lacked proper weapons,
that his voice, colour and body were no match for the civil-
ised concepts of theatre. This is an endemic evil that cannot
be dissolved by professional hatred or by bitter flaunting
of his race. In his encounter with a tawdry history he was
shaken by judgments of this sort:

> There has been romance, but it has been the romance of
> pirates and outlaws. The natural graces of life do not show
> themselves under such conditions. There has been no saint in
> the West Indies since Las Casas, no hero unless philo-Negro en-
> thusiasm can make one out of Toussaint. There are no people
> there in the true sense of the word, with a character and pur-
> pose of their own.

This is the tone used of canaille, but it is canaille who,
in exasperation at this truth, begin revolutions.
The pride of the colonial in the culture of his mother
country was fiercer than her true children's because the

colonial feared to lose her. The most conservative and prejudiced redoubts of imperialism are in those who have acquired that patina through strenuous reverence: her judges and, ironically enough, her artists. My generation since its colonial childhood had no true pride but awe. We had not yet provided ourselves with heroes, and when the older heroes went out of fashion, or were stripped, few of us had any choice but to withdraw into a cave where we could scorn those who struggled in the heat. Change was too subterranean for us to notice. Our melodramatic instincts demanded sudden upheavals, and found nothing in the Roman patience of legal reforms. We became infuriated at the banal demands of labourer and peasant. We romanticised the poor. But the last thing which the poor needed was the idealisation of their poverty. No play could be paced to the repetitive, untheatrical patience of hunger and unemployment. Hunger produces enervation of will and knows one necessity. Although in very few of the islands are people reduced to such a state, the empire of hunger includes work that is aimed only at necessities. It's inevitable that any playwright, knowing that this is his possible audience, will not be concerned with deprivation as his major theme. So the sparse body of West Indian theatre still feeds on the subject of emaciation and what it produces: rogues, drunkards, madmen, outcasts, and sets against this the pastoral of the peasant. Its comedy begins with the premise that all are starved or deprived, or defend themselves from being further deprived by threats. Hunger induces its delirium, and it is this fever for heroic examples that can produce the glorification of revenge.

Yet revenge is a kind of vision. The West Indian mind

historically hung-over, exhausted, prefers to take its revenge in nostalgia, to narrow its eyelids in a schizophrenic daydream of an Eden that existed before its exile. Its fixation is for the breasts of a nourishing mother, and this is true not only of the generations of slaves' children, but of those brought here through indigence or necessity, in fact, through the threat of hunger. But the communities maintain a half-brother relationship threatened by jealousies and suspicion. There is more romance in anthropology than there is in ordinary life, and our quarrels about genealogy, our visionary plays about the noble savage remain provincial, psychic justifications, strenuous attempts to create identity; yet there is nothing atavistic about our desires except that easy nostalgia which Hearne has described. Once we have lost our wish to be white we develop a longing to become black, and those two may be different, but are still careers. "The status of native is a nervous condition introduced and maintained by the settler among colonised people *with their consent*," says Sartre, introducing Fanon, and the new black continues that condition. His crimes are familial, litigious, his hatred is turned inward. The law is all he can remember of his past. Slaves, the children of slaves, colonials, then pathetic, unpunctual nationalists, what have we to celebrate? First, we have not wholly sunk into our own landscapes, as one gets the feeling at funerals that our bodies make only light, unlasting impressions on our earth. It is not an earth that has been fed long with the mulch of cultures, with the cycles of tribalism, feudalism, monarchy, democracy, industrialisation. Death, which fastens us to the earth, remains pastoral or brutish, because no single corpse contributes to some tiered concept of a past. Everything is immediate, and this immediacy means over-breeding, illegitimacy, migration without remorse. The sprout casually stuck in the soil. The depth of being rooted is related to the shallowness of racial despair. The migratory West Indian feels rootless on his own earth, chafing at its beaches.

V

> *Whosoever will, whosoever will . . .*
> *Hear the loving Father*
> *Call the wanderer home*
> *Whosoever will may come . . .*
> Salvation Army Hymn

A gas lamp startles the sidewalk and catches like fire-edged coals the black faces of men in white, martial uniforms, dilating the dun goatskin of the big bass drum, throwing its tireless radiance as far as our balcony across the street, changing the crossroads of Mary Ann Street and the Chaussée to a stage crossed by shadows. The recruiting patrol was Protestant, and their beat, thudding so loud that the stars shook, was to drum an army of Catholics into service by the joy of their performance, to arrest whoever paused, to draw children in a ring around the lantern-light until there would be more than spectators: an unheard army singing in the pebbled backyards, in the jalousied upstairs bedrooms whose moonlit linen would have to wait. And if there were, too rarely, a brass cornet played by some silver-headed English adjutant, its high note striking sparks from the tin roofs, then a kind of marching would begin, but one that kept the native beat. Yet, like the long, applauded note, joy soared further from two pale children staring from their upstairs window, wanting to march with that ragged, barefooted crowd, but who could not because they were not black and poor, until for one of them, watching the shouting, limber congregation, that difference became a sadness, that sadness rage, and that longing to share their lives ambition, so that at least one convert was made. They were the shadows of his first theatre, just as, at Christmas in the streets the Devil in red underwear, with a hemp beard, a pitchfork and a monstrously packed crotch, backed by a molasses-smeared chorus of imps, would perform an elaborate black mass of resurrection at the street corners. He and his brother were already creating their own little theatre, "little men" made from twigs enacting melodramas of hunting and escape, but of cowboys and gangsters, not of overseers and maroons. On the verandah, with his back to the street, he began marathon poems on Greek heroes which ran out of breath, lute songs, heroic tragedies, but these rhythms, the Salvation Army parodies, the Devil's Christmas songs, and the rhythms of the street itself were entering the pulse-beat of the wrist.

I do not remember if they played at savages with their cheap puppets; certainly poverty was never dramatised but what must have come out of all this later was a guilt; a guilt as well as an envy. One could envy the poor then, their theatre where everything was possible, sex, obscenity, absolution, freedom, and not only the freedom to wander barefoot, but the freedom made from necessity, the freedom to hack down forests, to hollow canoes, to hunt snakes, to fish,

and to develop bodies made of tarred rope that flung off
beads of sweat like tightened fish-lines. There were other
theatres too. There was the theatre of degeneracy. Not
clouds of heroes, but of flies. The derelicts who mimed their
tragedies, the lunatics who every day improvised absurd
monodramas, blasphemous, scabrous monologues, satirists,
cripples, alcoholics, one transvestite, one reprieved murderer, several hunched, ant-crazy old women, including one
who paused in the middle of the street to address her feet
and reprimand the sun, one other fantasist dressed in black
silk hat, gloves, frock-coat, soiled spats and cane, another, a
leg lost bucking like a sailor, one parched, ravaged poet,
ex-athlete and piano-fiend; all towns are full of them, but
their determined, self-destructive desolation was performed. Johnnie Walker, Pepsi-Cola, Wild Bill Hickok,
Cat-Strangler, Fowl-Thief, Baz the Dead, Wax-me-all-
over-except-my-balls, Bull-voiced Deighton, Submarine the
Bum-Boatman, the untranslatable N'Homme Mama Mi-
grains (your louse's mother's man), Lestrade sallow and
humped like a provincial Sherlock Holmes, Estefine Manger Farine, and the inestimable Greene, Bap, Joumard and
Vorn.

And there were vampires, witches, gardeurs, masseurs
(usually a fat black foreign-smelling blackness, with gold-
rimmed spectacles), not to mention the country where the
night withheld a whole, unstarred mythology of flaming,
shed skins. Best of all, in the lamplit doorway at the creaking hour, the stories sung by old Sidone, a strange croaking
of Christian and African songs. The songs, mainly about
lost children, were sung in a terrible whine. They sang of
children lost in the middle of a forest, where the leaves'

ears pricked at the rustling of devils, and one did not know if to weep for the first two brothers of every legend, one strong, the other foolish. All these sank like a stain. And taught us symmetry. The true folk tale concealed a structure as universal as the skeleton, the one armature from Br'er Anancy to King Lear. It kept the same digital rhythm of three movements, three acts, three moral revelations, whether it was the tale of three sons or of three bears, whether it ended in tragedy or happily ever after. It had sprung from hearthside or lamplit hut-door in an age when the night outside was a force, inimical, infested with devils, wood-demons, a country for the journey of the soul, and any child who has heard its symmetry chanted would want to retell it when he was his own story-teller, with the same respect for its shape. The apparent conservatism of West Indian fiction, whether in fiction or in theatre, is not an imitative respect for moulds, but a memory of that form.

Years later in another island you have formed a company so intimate that they have become limbs, extensions of your sensibility. You are rehearsing *The Blacks,* and you begin to see that their minds, whatever the variety of their education, are baffled by this challenge of the absurd. They resist the emphatic gaiety of that dance at the edge of the abyss. Its despair is another mimicry. They have the confused vitality of beginners, and like all beginners they are humanists. Presented with Gênet's black and white dumb-show, its first half a negative, its second half a print, the actors hesitate to recognise their images.

It may have to do with those subterranean charges that explode in their faces, for the play is mined with blinding flashes that cause a painful laughter. They catch, sidewise in the mirror of another's face, images of what they have feared, projections of their own caricatures. But their genius is not violent, it is comic. The play becomes less a satire and more a Carnival. Their joy is its root. The madness of surrealism means nothing to their sensibility, and this lack is not a question of culture, but simply that their minds refuse to be disfigured. An actor feels a play through the nerves, not through the brain, and his instinct is to feel his body move, to tingle towards gesture, towards promiscuous exchange with fellow actors. It is not that they do not understand the absurd, but that they cannot enjoy its mincing, catamite dances of death. But as their society avoids truths, as their Carnival is a noise that fears everything, too many of the actors avoid the anguish of self-creation. So one closes West Indian plays in despair. Closes, and reopens them in the hope that the last, twilight-sodden sigh is mistaken and that morning will vigorously bring a stronger, exhilarating despair; not a despair that belongs to others, but a truly tragic joy. It is our damnation to sigh not only for the amenities of civilization, its books, its women, its theatres, but also for its philosophies; and when revenge is the mode and a black *angst* fashionable, or when deprivation is made a cult-guilt of our artists, we find ourselves enraged. We imitate the images of ourselves.

An actor rises to a text and his tongue stumbles on words that have less immediacy than his dialect and he collapses, or fakes difficulty, abashed. He confronts proper speech as his body once confronted certain "inflexible" classic gestures. He stands torn between the wish to amuse or to illuminate his people.

For imagination and body to move with original instinct,

we must begin again from the bush. That return journey, with all its horror of rediscovery, means the annihilation of what is known. Some of our poets have pretended that journey, but with an itinerary whose resting points are predetermined. On such journeys the mind will discover what it chooses, and what these writers seek, like refugees raking debris, are heirlooms to dignify an old destitution. Even this destitution, carefully invoked, is pastoral. But if the body could be reduced once more to learning, to a rendering of things through groping mnemonic fingers, a new theatre could be made, with a delight that comes in roundly naming its object. Out of it, with patience, new reverberations would come. Yet this too, the haemophilic twilight said, with its sapping of the will before rehearsals: "Bourgeois, safe in a vague, pastoral longing, you pretend to re-enter the bush, to imitate the frenzy of ancestral possession, your soul, with a fetid dampness, drifts between two temples, and the track to the grove is fenced." You despise the banal vigour of a future, where the folk art, the language, the music, like the economy, will accommodate itself to the centre of power which is foreign, where people will simplify themselves to be clear, to be immediately apprehensible to the transient. The lean, sinewy strength of the folk-dance has been fattened and sucked into the limbo of the night-club, the hotel cabaret, and all the other prostitutions of a tourist culture: before you is the vision of a hundred Havanas and mini-Miamis, and who dares tell their Tourism Boards and Cultural Development Committees that the blacks in bondage at least had the resilience of their dignity, a knowledge of their degradation, while their descendants have gone both flaccid and colourful, covering their suffering with artificial rage or commercial elation? Even the last one among us who knows the melodies of the old songs fakes his African, becoming every season, by Kodak exposure of his cult, a phony shaman, a degraded priest. The urge towards the metropolitan language was the same as political deference to its centre, but the danger lay in confusing, even imitating the problems of the metropolis by pretensions to its power, its styles, its art, its ideas, and its concept of what we are. The core of this conflict was whether only a true city, by which one meant the metropolitan power, could nourish a theatre, or whether our cities, lacking all power, could be called cities at all. Ironically enough, the theatre at the heart of the metropolis was trying to reduce power to tribal simplicities of penitence and celebration, while our politics, as well as our arts, strove for sophistry even to the point of imitated decadence. For our frustrated avant-gardists and our radicals there was neither enough power nor decadence to justify experiment; they missed our de Sade, our Grotowski or the madness of an Artaud. While others, reactionaries in dashikis, screamed for the pastoral vision, for a return to nature over the loudspeaker. It was always the fate of the West Indian to meet himself coming back, and he would only discover the power of simplicity, the graces of his open society after others had embraced it as a style.

VI

*Hence our confirmed lack of culture is astonished by
certain grandiose anomalies; for example, on an island
without any contact with modern civilization, the mere
passage of a ship carrying only healthy passengers may
provoke the sudden outbreak of diseases unknown on
that island but a specialty of nations like our own:
shingles, influenza, grippe, rheumatism, sinusitis, poly-
neuritis, etc.*

Artaud: *The Theatre and Its Double*

I try to divert my concentration from that mesmeric
gritted oyster of sputum on the concrete floor of a tin-
roofed shed in back of a choirmaster's house, half shango-
chapel, half Presbyterian country vestry, but there are two
people circling that filthy asterisk in search of a gramophone needle which the choirmaster bewails that he bought
just, just this morning, with our bewilderment before the
screw-ups of technology, as if the gramophone vindictively
insisted that their voices should be enough and had mag-
isterially withdrawn its contribution. The women of the
choir are dressed in the standard imitation frippery of
Mexican or Venezuelan peasants: black skirts appliquéd
with cushion-sized flowers, low-necked, lace-edged cotton
bodices, and prim shoes, the plainest of the women with,
unless argument is dominating memory, a lurid bloody
hibiscus in her greased hair. The men are modestly dressed.
Onstage, they might wear the three-quarter-length cotton
trousers of the peon, and, if they were dancers, rainbow-

rippled sleeves, more feminine than androgynous. Piquancy, charm have already emasculated those. Their dances have been refined to a female essence, a grinning fragility, suffocating as cheap perfume, their jetés and turns false as the coquetry of the women whose sex at least pullulates with the appeal of sweating crotches, while the men, the finer-boned the better, can offer nothing but their tightened, scrotum-packed costumes and witty backsides. Leave that alone. It's whoredom and they will be paid. We are gathered here for something votive, and the choir-men have a protestant demureness, an inward smiling modesty.

But the night degenerates from decency to decency, offering, as though they were the shredded flesh and tree-sapped blood of the Saviour, the little cakes, sweets, thinned drinks and papery crisps of processed corn, plantain, potato, even the last vegetal gods dried and distributed. Then they begin to sing. They sing from what they have learnt from movies. They have acquired presentation, style. This consists of the women swaying gently from side to side without quite holding the edges of their flared skirts, like a child reciting, swaying their pressed heads, rounding their mouths, flirting with their eyes, and bowing, Jesus! bowing neatly, with the practised modesty of professionals, except that the bow does not quite work like the professional's wry, screw-you-if-you-didn't-like-it smile, no, it contains the shrunken pride of the Community Centre, the ambition of social achievement. The sour constipated earth is hard as cement. Once their heels, like the heels of the drummer's on the palms carcass of the drum, would have made it resound. The worst song, the most sincerely sung, is an original, an anthem to the nation. The sentiments are infantile (though children are innocent of patriotism), the words and phrasing execrable. But the passion with which it is sung is its most desolating aspect. Furiously ungrammatical, emphatically crude, but patinaed with grace. It smells as soon as it is aired. It sickens everything, as crude and as natural as that dusted globule of splayed spit that has become the itch of your whole body. The flashing banana leaves, the thick, hot air, the thick, black voices straining for refinement, all these are mixed in one hallucination, slowly stunning into acceptance, if one is not to feel the old madness creaking the skull open again; the jet of spit on the gritty cement floor repeats, converts itself into saying, well it is all very touching and simple, it is sincere, it is real. Those dusty banana fronds are real, the gold teeth, and their thin gold watches, and the careful articulation of their small talk; and it is only you who are unnecessary, unreal. To create your reality, you must become part of them, spit, applaud, touch, eat with and sing with them, but what really sings in the dark hole of the heart is hollowness, what screams is something lost, something so embarrassed, like an animal that abandons its dying image in its cub, and moves deeper into bush. They are glad to see it go. I can feel it gone. It is gone in the precise signalling of those fine, fixed stars. Gone, with an odour of choking talc and perfume. Later, after the smiling Minister goes, and the distinguished guests, of which you are one, the drumming and the true singing jerked alive by the rum and the furiously sweating night, all that straining after the old truth may begin, but the bored animal has gone to sleep. It is too late. Too late.

VII

The only escape was drama.
V. S. Naipaul

All these are affirmations of identity, however forced. Our bodies think in one language and move in another, yet it should have become clear, even to our newest hybrid, the black critic who accuses poets of betraying dialect, that the language of exegesis is English, that the manic absurdity would be to give up thought because it is white. In our self-tortured bodies we confuse two graces: the dignity of self-belief and the courtesies of exchange. For us the ragged, untutored landscape seems as uncultured as our syntax.

So, like that folk-choir, my first poems and plays expressed this yearning to be adopted, as the bastard longs for his father's household. I saw myself legitimately prolonging the mighty line of Marlowe, of Milton, but my sense of inheritance was stronger because it came from estrangement. I would learn that every tribe hoards its culture as fiercely as its prejudices, that English literature, even in the theatre, was hallowed ground and trespass, that colonial literatures could grow to resemble it closely, but could never be considered its legitimate heir. There was folk poetry, colonial poetry, Commonwealth verse, etc., and their function, as far as their mother country was concerned, was filial and tributary. I sighed up a continent of envy when I studied English literature, yet, when I tried to talk as I wrote, my voice sounded affected or too raw.

The tongue became burdened, like an ass trying to shift its load. I was taught to trim my tongue as a particular tool which could as easily have been ordered from England as an awl or a chisel, and that eloquence which I required of its actors was against the grain of their raw and innocent feeling. This kind of aggression increased an egotism which can pass for genius. I was thus proclaimed a prodigy because I insisted on a formality which had nothing to do with their lives. It made me believe that twilight had set me apart and naturally I arrived at the heresy that landscape and history had failed me.

VIII

And in the end the age was handed
the sort of shit that it demanded.
                    Hemingway

His defiance now a mania driven to the pitch where only vision was real, the leader would pray: Let me help others and be merciless to myself. But the torment of all self-appointed schizoid saints is that they enact their opposite. Thus, in his case also, strength of public purpose fed on private deterioration. So even righteous anger was corruptible; his self-sacrifice contained a fury that was really revenge. He alone would roll the Sisyphean boulder uphill, even if it cracked his backbone. The fuel of his ambition was no longer love but the ecstasy of nervous exhaustion and drink. This ecstasy, like all power, was heady, brutal and corrupting. Its rages were forgiven because they were abstract, but every explosion eroded and demeaned the soul. He began to imagine treacheries where there was only misunderstanding. Nothing less than their self-blinded obedience would satisfy him. He had been warned of this madness, and true enough, paranoia progressed with every inch of slope cleared. But who would help should he let go the stone, or, when he rested, help prop it with scotching heels and groaning back? On mornings of fitful remorse, after he had abused the actors, he would clinically study the symptoms: the blinding anger, the cirrhosis of suspicion, the heart-sickness of failure. Perhaps these were the exactions of courage, but they left his skin prickling, his head roaring with amnesia, his ego massively inflamed. Such fury was suicidal. It had broken, even killed a few, but he saw each breakdown as revenge. Well, as they said in this country, who send him? There were fights with actors coarser than anything imaginable, where exasperation reduced to tears, whose violence annihilated all self-respect.

But even these explosions were better than the myth of the organic, ineradicable tsetse, the numbing fly in the mythically different blood, the myth of the uncreative, parasitic, malarial nigger, the marsh-numbed imagination that is happiest in mud. Anger was better than nothing, better than that embittered affection with which each called the other nigger. They moved from hall to basement to shed, and the parallel of all this was the cliché of the destitute, digs-deprived emigrant out on the grey streets; only this was supposed to be home, a launching place, a base of sorties and retreats from failure.

After a time invisible lianas strangle our will. Every night some area in the rapidly breeding bush of the mind would be cleared, an area where one could plan every inch of advance by firelight. Yes, the director was developing a Christ-complex, a readiness for suffering and betrayal, a Salvation Army theatre for the half-literate, the ambitious, the frustrated. What sustained him was a phrase from child-hood—"Wherever two or three are gathered in Thy name" —and this increased in Him, when only a handful of disciples showed up at rehearsals, an arrogant despair. It was more than a romance with the nobleness of failure, for his persistence was being complimented. One was now praised by those of one's generation who had given up art and whose realism comprised "integrity" and "public good," a new, brown meritocracy, who had accepted the limitations of their society, but whose solicitude concealed insult.

You had to endure their respect, their vapid, reassuring smiles at parties and at those dinners you were summoned to to electrify with abuse. You went, knowing how dead they would be behind eyes that, repeated in the Sunday features, showed the nervous belligerence of graduates. They were eyes that denied their power, bright with charity. The idea of a theatre and the possibilities of their cities bored them, because they had accepted failure as logic. Duty had delineated itself to him—to transform the theatrical into theatre, to qualify the subtlety between a gift and a curse, but this was a society fed on an hysterical hallucination, that believed only the elaborate frenzy now controlled by the State. But Carnival was as meaningless as the art of the actor confined to mimicry. And now the intellectuals, courting and fearing the mass, found values in it that they had formerly despised. They apotheosised

34

the folk form, insisting that calypsos were poems. Their programme, for all its pretext to change, was a manual for stasis, because they wanted politically to educate the peasant yet leave him intellectually unsoiled; they baffled him with schisms and the complexities of Power while insisting that he needed neither language nor logic, telling him that what he yearned for was materialistic, imitative and corrupt, while all his exhorters made sure that their wives were white, their children brown, their jobs inviolate.

No, for the colonial artist the enemy was not the people, or the people's crude aesthetic which he refined and orchestrated, but the enemy was those who had elected themselves as protectors of the people, frauds who cried out against indignities done to the people, who urged them to acquire pride which meant abandoning their individual dignity, who cried out that black was beautiful like transmitters from a different revolution without explaining what they meant by beauty, all of these had emerged from nowhere, suddenly, a different, startling "canaille." Their rough philosophies were meant to coarsen every grace, to demean courtesy, to brook no debate, their fury artificially generated by an imitation of even metropolitan anger, now. *Tristes, tristes tropiques!* We had come from an older, wiser, sadder world that had already exorcised those devils, but these were calling out the old devils to political use. Witch-doctors of the new left with imported totems. The people were ready to be betrayed again.

So with fatigued conceit he realised that to continue he would have to sustain the hallucination that the world revolved around him. He lied to himself by cherishing their devotion; he found not shame but promise in their near-literacy, because he had accepted this role of martyr. It gave him the perversity of remaining obscure while desiring fame, of being wrecked on a rock while hoping that his whirlpool was the navel of the world. It was he who thought for them, who had salted their minds with subtleties that they might have been happier to ignore.

Exasperation nourished him. It urged him towards texts that were fantastical or violent, plays with the purgation of revenge. All he knew in those moods was that he wanted a theatre whose language could be that of the drowning, a gibberish of cries. It was fearful to carry that world within him alone. The contagion of that madness electrified them when they were all drunk or drunk on elation. Now he watched what he feared: the revolt that settles for security, the feeling in those still inadequate minds that they were message-bearers. They might subjugate their bodies to everything, but every growth of power exposed their deficiencies. When they were excellent in gesture they were thick in speech, they could rarely explain or repeat what instinct clarified, and now a few would approach him with frightening requests: to understand the technique of theatre as if it were something different from what their bodies instinctually practised, for better speech when theirs had vigour that was going out of English. Now they wanted to be as good as others. Good enough to go abroad. They showed that cursed, colonial hunger for the metropolis. The desertions had begun.

One does not lament the twenty years spent in trying to create this reality of a theatre, nor could one have contempt for its successes and the honours that "recognition" has brought, but the ceremony of reward is as misguided as the supposedly defunct system of long service, by which is meant self-sacrifice, for the reward itself acknowledges the odds which its donors have perpetuated by regarding art as monastic, by honouring the spirit after the body is worn down by the abrasions of indifference, by regarding the theatre as civic martyrdom. The theatre is a crass business, and money is better than medals. They thought in memorials, pensions, plaques. It is in that sense that nothing has changed, that one is still imprisoned in the fear of abandoning talent to despair. The messianic role is no longer flattering. It tires, it infuriates, it is sick of hearing "what would happen if . . ." It is not deceived by the noises of the State when it proclaims the power of folk-culture, nor by the wily patronage of merchants. Without knowing it the folk forms had become corrupted by politics. Their commercialisation is now beyond anger, for they have become part of the climate, the art of the brochure.

What to do then? Where to turn? How to be true? If one went in search of the African experience, carrying the luggage of a few phrases and a crude map, where would it end? We had no language for the bush and there was a conflicting grammar in the pace of our movement. Out of this only an image came. A band of travellers, in their dim outlines like explorers who arrived at the crest of a dry, grassy ridge. There the air was heady, sharp, threading the lungs finely, with the view hidden, then levelling off to the tin-roofed, toy town of his childhood. The sense of hallucination increased with the actuality of every detail, from the chill, mildly shivering blades of hill-grass, from their voices abrupted by the wind, the duality of time, past and present piercingly fixed as if the voluble puppets of his childhood were now frighteningly alive. A few pointed out the house with its pebbled backyard where they had had their incarnations a quarter of a century ago, the roofs from which that martial cornet had struck its sparks, while some turned towards the lush, dark-pocketed valleys of banana with their ochre tracks and canted wooden huts from whose kitchens, at firelight, the poetry which they spoke had come, and further on, the wild, white-lined Atlantic coast with an Africa that was no longer home, and the dark, oracular mountain dying into mythology. It was as if, with this sinewy, tuned, elate company, he was repaying the island an ancestral debt. It was as if they had arrived at a view of their own bodies walking up the crest, their bodies tilted slightly forward, a few survivors. It was not a vision but a memory, though its detail was reduced, as in dreams and in art. But knowing the place could not tell me what it meant. There was only this reduced image of real actors on a real, windy grass ridge, which was, of course, the Morne overlooking the harbour of Castries and the banana fields to windward, on the very spine of Saint Lucia. Perhaps it meant that I had brought us home. The cycle finished. Perhaps the ridge was a point of rest. Perhaps achievement. We would have to descend again. To leave that clear, heady air of achievement and go down again. I was with and not with them. I watched them but was not among them. They were they. They were there. They needed no more enthusiasm from the good guide, but for all the exhilaration of that air, I did not know where else to take them now, except up to the crest again, repeating the one image like a film. Henceforth no struggle, only the repetition of little victories. Had one closed their hopes or opened them? There was a value in darkness, in the cultivation of obscurity. On that little summit, where the air is spring-nipped or autumn-chilling, I may have lost them.

The last image is of a rain-flushed dawn, after a back-breaking night of filming, in a slowly greying field where the sea wind is like metal on the cheek. In the litter of the field, among black boxes of equipment and yellow, sleekly wet tarpaulins, stands a shawled girl caught in that gesture which abstractedly gathers cloth to shoulder, her black hair lightly lifting, the tired, pale skin flushed, lost in herself and the breaking camp. She was white, and that no longer mattered. Her stillness annihilated years of anger. His heart thanked her silently from the depth of exhaustion, for she was one of a small army of his dream. She was a vessel caught at the moment of departure of their Muse, her clear vacancy the question of a poem which is its own answer. She was among the sentries who had watched till dawn.

I am bound within them, neither knowing which is liana or trunk, which is the parasite, which is the host, since if I dared to confess to ambition I could be using them, and they the same. All their betrayals are quarrels with the self, their pardonable desertions the inevitable problem of all island artists: the choice of home or exile, self-realisation or spiritual betrayal of one's country. Travelling widens this breach. Choice grows more melodramatic with every twilight. When twenty years ago we imagined cities devoted neither to power nor to money but to art, one had the true vision. Everything else has been the sweated blurring of a mirror in which the people might have found their true reflection.

Petit Valley
Trinidad
February 1970

The Sea at Dauphin

FOR ERROL HILL

*The sea doth wash away
all human ills.*

Euripides

CHARACTERS

AFA, a fisherman

GACIA, a fisherman

AUGUSTIN, Afa's mate

HOUNAKIN, an old East Indian

A PRIEST

JULES, a boy

WOMEN OF DAUPHIN

(The play was originally produced by Errol Hill for the Whitehall Players in 1954. It was performed by the Theatre Workshop at the Basement Theatre, Bretton Hall, Port of Spain, on January 7, 1966, with the following cast: Ralph Campbell as AFA; Claude Reid as GACIA; Geddes Jennings as AUGUSTIN; Albert LeVeau as HOUNAKIN; Peter Bruce as the PRIEST; Inniss Vincent as JULES; and Constance Allsopp, Grace Walke, Leone Campbell, Janet Stanley and Lucita Baptiste as the WOMEN OF DAUPHIN.)

The Scene

A Windward island in the West Indies, on its nerve-wracked Atlantic coast, two hours from sunrise. Age-grey morning before the fishermen file, gum-eyed, hitching their trousers, to the latrine on the beach's spit in the bay. Nothing on the beach now so early, except a sail, patched square from used flour sacks, washing its slack cheeks with the wind. In the sleep-tightened village a dog is coughing among the lanes, then by the grey false light of daybreak a fisherman comes down the littered beach, barefooted, wrapped in a moth-riddled sweater against the October cold, carrying a dented tin, coils of marlin twine, and a bamboo pole. He wears a cap with the braid shredded, and pants quilted with patches. In the bow of a canoe that protrudes from a clump of stunted grapes he rests the pail down, then the rod, picks dead leaves floating in the bilge of the boat, then squints unwillingly at the bad weather; fiddles in his cap for a butt, lights it against the wind, then rubs it out. He sits on a stone near the canoe. Its bow is lettered with the words *Our Daily Bread.* This man is AFA, over forty, and gritty-tempered as he unpacks the twine, mumbling, and thins it out between finger and thumb. Soon another fisherman, GACIA, stale drunk, twice as tattered, in his old constable's cloak comes dead-footed down the beach.

GACIA

Bon matin, boug.

45

AFA

Matin, Gacia, *bon matin.* Wind hard, eh? [*Looking at the sky*] Wind still savage.

GACIA

Ay, *oui,* the cold will drop, but this just half the wind. The next half in the sea back-pocket, by Sablisse. Where Augustin?

AFA

You know Augustin. Augustin is his woman blanket. Where Debel?

GACIA

Debel? Debel sick. [*Imitates a man vomiting*] *Rhum.*

AFA

You see, cousin? Rum is a bad wife.

GACIA

But you must sleep with it. Debel finish. Between him and his woman not much leave. He should die, since to beg is worse. [*Shivering*] I don't even take my little coffee yet. [*Looks at sky*] Two weeks now, this sea whiter than spit, two weeks is rain.

AFA

It white like the time when Bolo drown. [*Points off-shore*] There so!

GACIA

Garçon, to see a next day so like when Bolo drown . . .
[*Shakes his head*] I remember . . .

AFA

But the sea forget.

GACIA

The sea do what it have to do, like wind, like birds. Like
me. Cigawette? [*Offers* AFA *a cigarette*] American.

AFA

[*Wiping his hands*] Merci . . . [*Looks at it*] Ay, ay, *boug.*
'Ous riche, a whole one? [*They laugh*] Is only natural for
wind to blow so hard, but to turn, and turn. You going
out, you one? The others, they making one with their
woman, only both of us two so stupid.

GACIA

It staying so for a next month, *compère,* and in all my life
I never see it more vex and it have many season, fishing
nasse, I see it bad; but never in a life, like this. But is work
or starve. They have many garden wash down in Fond
River. We curse, *compère.* God forget us . . . *Bonne
chance* . . . the sail have a hole . . . [*Goes off, singing*]

AFA

Eh-heh, I know, I know . . .

> [GACIA *exits.* AFA *stands to watch him go, impatiently
> stamping his foot. He is fixing the twine angrily when a*

47

*yell from the hill stops him. AFAaaaaaaah ooooh, AFAo-
oooooy, and suddenly a lithe agitated young man breaks
through the bushes, stuffing his merino into his pants,
and chattering in the cold. The young man is* AUGUSTIN,
AFA's *mate. He throws his things in the canoe and hugs
himself]*

AUGUSTIN

Bon matin, bon matin, Admiral, *Bon Dieu, Jesi Marie La
Vierge en ciel, mwen fwette,* it making cold, woy!

AFA

Is time for this old man to come, morning break and you
can't smell this wind? Gacia pass now so going for his canoe.

AUGUSTIN

You mean Gacia one? Make me aid you with the twine.
Gacia one? Where Debel?

AFA

Is sick. Is time for this old man, *oui.*

AUGUSTIN

Debel sick? Rum and sea water not a good drink. Ay, where
you going?

AFA

Look! Just now sun will rise, and wind working already.
And fish waiting for nobody is working late. Mind you foot
by the hook there!

AUGUSTIN

You have a cigawette? It making cold.

48

A F A

Not now, not now, when you want one for true. [*Exasperated*] Look, Monsieur Augustin, this fish you know it have now fifteen years, does wait for people line to hook them up? I tired use me tongue and tell you, don't care how you drinking in Samuel café, or talking how you brave in front of them Dauphin women, work is work, and sea and I don't sleep. I tell you when you pass, pass for the old man. Where he is now? Where this old man?

A U G U S T I N

Last night in Samuel café, when white rum scald you tongue, is not you tell this old man he can come? Not you what have water in you eyes from Samuel onions, and cry on the old man shoulder?

A F A

Well, today I feel to say *non. Non!* Last night did drunk. Everybody drunk, you ask me when I did drunk. This morning I have sense, and so is *non, non!*

A U G U S T I N

The old man is my godfather!

A F A

What a man, to drown he godfather!

A U G U S T I N

Is my godfather, and I want to drown him is my business! Piece of the canoe is mine you know.

49

AFA

Bien! So is for that you doing you don't know what season
sea have now, as if is not September pass that Bolo drown,
there self, so close you can hear scissor bird cutting the
wind, you can hear gaulin feather fall on rock. Forty years,
quarante, I work this water, and this is one bitch wind on
Dauphin side today!

AUGUSTIN

[*Sitting down*] *Eh bien,* we bound to go, Admiral?

AFA

Eh-heh, we bound to go, because nobody going; when is
nice even woman going.

AUGUSTIN

Fish know wind too, Afa, come bet today fish hiding?

AFA

Eh bien, stay home and make garden with you woman!

AUGUSTIN

Make garden! *Cooyon!* Is only you one who know current?
Is only you who have need to work like nigger? Only you
who brave? They have bigger than you on the sand under
the sea, they have brave we don't hear yet is food for fish.
Cooyon!

AFA

Look, give me my respect you hear! I know you since you

wetting this same pants you have; piece of the canoe is yours but gi' me my respect or we mashing up now self!

AUGUSTIN

Tiens! We always mashing up, just like you and you woman.

AFA

I have no woman.

AUGUSTIN

Don't have no woman only? You don't have no love, no time, no child, you have a hole where man heart should be, you have no God, no dog, no friend, that is why Dauphin fraid you, because you always enrage, and nobody will give you help of the hand, so you make it, live with it . . . Woman will leave you till you dead.

AFA

Look, eh!

AUGUSTIN

And when you dead, who will cry? Only blind Batal is peeling onions for Samuel on a bench behind the café, and a few grains of rain. Not me, not Gacia. And at your wake, if they so stupid to have wake for fool like you, women saying only "They had this man Afa, who greedy make fisherman, a man that beat his woman, that have no love, no mercy, no compassion!" I pass the old man *ajoupa* before daybreak, the house eyes close, and he cannot sleep, he crying in the making dark, making ehhhh like dog, and the dog self watching him, waiting to die. I run here fast to tell you wait. —But why I talking to you? . . . [AFA *has turned away. Silence*] You fix the hole was in the bottom of the canoe?

AFA

Ah, God, you hear?

AUGUSTIN

You fix the hole, pal? *Doux, doux*, ay, papa, give Agos a little kiss . . . you vex? Pal, pal, . . . you fix the hole was in the bottom of . . .

AFA

I bring the *calebasse* to bail. The old man have to bail.

AUGUSTIN

He have a old hurt in his back, you know that?

AFA

So when we pass Point Jesu, and where water making white after Sablisse, I must take my two eyes from the wind, and my hand from the boat to rub his back?

AUGUSTIN

Bon Dieu, Afa, Sablisse? Why we going so far, and you can hear sea grinding his teeth in the making dark? . . . *'Ous malice*, Afa, *malice, malice* . . .

AFA

Malice! Compassion! What it have in this morning before

sun even wipe his eye, that I must take this dirty tongue from you, eh? When I did working your age with Bolo, you think I could show my teeth in disrespect? And this new thing, compassion? Where is compassion? Is I does make poor people poor, or this sea vex? Is I that put rocks where should dirt by Dauphin side, man cannot make garden grow? Is I that swell little children belly with bad worm, and woman to wear clothes white people use to wipe their foot? In my head is stone, and my heart is another, and without stone, my eyes would burst for that, would look for compassion on woman belly. I born and deading in this coast that have no compassion to grow food for children, no fish enough to buy new sail, no twine. Every day sweat, sun, and salt, and night is salt and sleep, and all the dead days pack away and stink, is Dauphin life. Not I who make it! So I must work the sea, that is my pasture, *garce*. If is compassion you want talk to the sea, ask it where Bolo bones, and Rafael, and friends I did have before you even born . . .

AUGUSTIN

So you not taking the old man?

AFA

What right a man is blind, two holes where had his eyes,
To work this sea? He think is land,
But you cannot plant it, the sea food does move,
And we must follow it. Today he will learn.

AUGUSTIN

Est-you taking him?

53

AFA

And Gacia pass Point Jesu long! *Gadez!* [*Smashes a calabash down in anger*] I have no time to wipe old man pants is frighten. He your godfather, and promise is to break. He coming, look at him coming, like piece of break-up stick. Not me in this thing!

AUGUSTIN

He can hear you.

AFA

Make him hear then!

AUGUSTIN

Do what you want! [*He sucks his teeth and starts to break up a twig*]

AFA

[*Loudly*] I say I not carrying nobody dead in my boat.

AUGUSTIN

Half the boat is mine.

AFA

I not carrying nobody dead in my half the boat, no old man on my shoulder. I know old man, dribbling in bed. Since Rama, his old woman dead, he think everybody must go round their face long like bamboo, the world work must stop because one old woman dead.

[*Now the old man for whom they have been waiting,* HOUNAKIN, *comes through the bushes. He is an old East*

*Indian, wrapped in almost rags, a green gourd in his
hand, carrying a cutlass. He wears a large straw hat, is
barefooted and walks painfully, squinting through narrow gummed eyes set in a face worn and cracked with
heat. He has overheard* AFA's *words. Now he waits with
the weary smile of the aged and near-deaf. He is suffering
from cataract and a cramp has stiffened one hand.* AFA
looks at him, then turns his back on the old man.
AUGUSTIN *gestures in despair]*

HOUNAKIN

[Coming forward wearily] Bon matin, mes messieurs. I
late . . .

AUGUSTIN

Bo' jou', papa.

HOUNAKIN

Ey, *M'sieu Afa, bon matin* . . .

AFA

Vieux corps! Sea is waiting for nobody, old not old. You
know how many *canot* gone? Sunrise is sun lying down
when fisherman late. You know early you go early you
come back, and fish must sell quick quick or fish rotten
fast, faster than old woman dead.

AUGUSTIN

[Rushes at him] Afa, *Sacré salop!*

AFA

[Facing him] Vini, vini, 'ti cooyon! Come!

55

[They stand facing each other, AUGUSTIN *with a stone]*

AUGUSTIN

You don't have no heart, [*Beating his breast*] you don't have no compassion, all you want is money, money, money, you same like a damn dog, a dog is what you are [*Getting nearer and nearer*] and your mother and your mother mother . . .

HOUNAKIN

Mes enfants, mes enfants! [*He stands between them*]

AFA

You want to fish is seventy years you have! Fisherman at seventy! But if you want it you doing like a boy is five years. And when Afa say four in the morning is four. All right, put down the cutlass in the boat, Houna, take off the stones in the *canot.* Augustin, take guard of the sail!

[AUGUSTIN *waits to pull down the sail*]

HOUNAKIN

God will bless you.

AFA

He taking long, old man. Ay! Augustin, I have a tin belonging Ratal in the bow, see if it there. [AFA *is helping* HOUNA-KIN *unballast the canoe*] You ever sail yet, papa? [HOUNAKIN *shakes his head*] Fish line? [HOUNAKIN *shakes his head*] Fish net? Nothing?

AUGUSTIN

No tin not there!

56

AFA

You never fishing?

HOUNAKIN

On jetty alone.

AFA

Is not the same thing.

HOUNAKIN

I know, captain.

AFA

You know why we taking out stone? Is more rough than you will see this sea again for many weeks, but we must go or belly full of wind, the *canot* must be fast and light to ride high white water, and if the pots have enough it will be heavy coming back. [*Turns and notices* AUGUSTIN *struggling with some twine*] The cord stick, you fool! He is the most ignorant nigger they have in the world. All he know is white rum and black woman. [*Now he helps* AUGUSTIN *furl the sail into the boat*] Repose your body under the wood-trees, old man, and watch sun breaking and guard us make *canot* ready for sea. The sea is very funny, papa. But it not making me laugh. Some say this sea is dead fisherman laughing. Some say is noise of all the fisherman woman crying. Sea in Dauphin never quiet. Always noise, noise. [*Pauses. Spits in the water. He leaves* AUGUSTIN *to fix the canoe and stands up over the old man*] It will not make you laugh, old man, every night it getting

57

whiter, and the birds running hungry on the rocks by
Maingot side.

AUGUSTIN

[*Pauses, looks up*] Old man don't frighten. You playing
with you death today, M'sieu Afa.

AFA

Since Bolo drown. Everybody say Boileau would never
drown. And Habal, Habal drowning there last year. And
in September is not Annelles, Gacia brother they find two
mile behind Dennery, one afternoon a boy catching crab,
walking, see him on sand, when all the *maître* boat looking
for him by Trou Pamphile, his body swell, and the boy
turn this thing with his foot and when he finish it was
Annelles, drown like what, like Raphael, and Boileau. Ay,
Augustin behind! *Derrière, derrière!* [*He changes the posi-
tion of the sail to the front of the canoe so that it now
projects from the bow*]

AUGUSTIN

[*Suddenly straightening up*] Afa!

AFA

What?

AUGUSTIN

Look Gacia coming back!

AFA

You lie . . .

58

[The fisherman, GACIA, who has passed earlier, now returns, dejected and soaked, trailing his pole, and beating his hat against his thighs. He stops when he sees the three men]

GACIA

They have some men who don't believe in nothing.
Unless is accident, who don't believe in love, unless
They breed their woman. Their head like Dauphin land,
All rock, and in the rock, worm, and in the worm head
Is only death. Afa, you are this man. Greedy
Will kill you. Old man, you choose a hard companion.
Go home and sleep, die in your hut.
This sea not make for men. God self can't sail it.

AFA

You going back?

GACIA

What you think? By Pointe it is like mad dog fighting.
Augustin ni un cigawette? All mine wet. [AFA *gives him his cigarette*] *Merci.*

AUGUSTIN

Is so bad truly?

GACIA

Go and see. You can take my fish too. [*Exit*]

AUGUSTIN

You hear what Gacia say? You hear old man? Afa?

AFA

We going still.

HOUNAKIN

À nous, à nous. I not afraid to die.

AUGUSTIN

You want to die! You old! I different. It have a lot I don't
do yet to die. Sun coming up, Afa, what to do?

HOUNAKIN

To die is once. *À nous.*

AUGUSTIN

[*Restraining him*] You mad? Wait, wait!

AFA

What happen now? Gacia is God?

AUGUSTIN

No. You is God.

AFA

We waiting for sun. This sea is Gacia woman no man must
touch it?

AUGUSTIN

The sea is the sea. [*He sits down and removes some bread
from a pocket, eating angrily*] I know you, Afa. All your life
is to be better than Bolo. You can't dead better than what
is dead. You want Dauphin and the whole coast to say Afa

60

was brave! Is when you drown you brave? You have no
respect for man, animal, sea or God.

AFA

This brave I have it come from many years,
Many years of sea, many years dolour.
That crack my face, and make my heart so hard.
If none going, then I will go alone.
If I don't have no love I don't have hate,
If I don't have woman, there is sea and sky.
God is a white man. The sky is his blue eye,
His spit on Dauphin people is the sea.
Don't ask me why a man must work so hard
To eat for worm to get more fat. Maybe I bewitch.
You never curse God, I curse him, and cannot die,
Until His time. This basin men call sea
Never get red for men blood it have. My turn is next.
I cannot sleep on land, like Gacia.
The land is hard, this Dauphin land have stone
Where it should have some heart. The sea
It have compassion in the end.

AUGUSTIN

[*Clapping in mockery*]

What it have across the sea?
You leave something in Africa?
Between there and Dauphin, ten thousand miles?
Is there you going?
And furthermore I can't swim.

61

AFA

[*To* HOUNAKIN] You can swim, papa?

HOUNAKIN

Non.

AFA

[*Sitting down suddenly, interested now that the canoe is equipped for work*] Tell me again, old man, why for you want to work the sea? And you so old? You never stay in your house and hear wind breaking wood-trees? You never go down on your two knees and thank the Virgin you never work this sea by Maingot side? Where is Habal, Raphael, Annelles, Boileau? Sun breaking, papa, talk fast. Where Boileau used to pull *canot* with his one hand? [HOUNAKIN, *frightened, cannot talk*] The onliest fisherman better than Boileau was Saint Pierre, both of them dead.

AUGUSTIN

You will not talk, old man? He want to die.

AFA

[*Rises*] Today is a good day. [*Businesslike*] *Alors!* All right. *Nous parti.* [*Giving orders expertly*] Augustin, we going; old man, we ready. [AUGUSTIN *pauses, looks seaward, then crosses himself.* AFA *and* AUGUSTIN *get ready to push the canoe, when the old man rises, dazed, and sits in it*] All right, Augustin, watch for the big wave. [*To the old man*] Get out the *canot*, old man, not time to sit. [*Turns away, his back to the old man*] When I say *poussez, poussez!* Ready?

AUGUSTIN

Come, papa. Not yet to sit down in the *canot*. Come, come
. . . [HOUNAKIN *is petrified;* AFA *turns round. His anger is
mounting*] *Sorti, sorti, vieux corps.* [*Touches* HOUNAKIN
on the shoulder] He is trembling.

AFA

What happen now?

AUGUSTIN

He is crying.

AFA

[*Striding over to the old man*] *Sorti, sorti,* papa, get up, get
up. [AUGUSTIN *lifts* HOUNAKIN'S *chin with his hand.* AFA
shakes him roughly] Get up, get up, papa, sun break long.

HOUNAKIN

Non, non, is cold, is cold . . .

AFA

[*Shaking him harder*] I say get up! Is making cold in this
hot sun! Is late!

AUGUSTIN

[*Pleading*] Papa, *sou 'plait, levez, levez!* [HOUNAKIN *is mumbling to himself*] He is like a man is dead, he is so cold . . .
papa.

AFA

[*Completely enraged*] *Ça c'est bettise,* man! Pull him out!

Haul the old man skin out the boat. Is not me kill his woman. You want me to pull him out? Smell him! Stink of white rum! He drunk! [*Begins to pull the old man*] Get out the backside boat, man time going!

AUGUSTIN

[*Raising his cutlass and weeping with rage*] Son of Man, Afa! Touch this old man once, once! *Avec un fois encore* and I cut you belly open and put a heart in it! *Touchez-lui! Touchez-lui!*

AFA

So is tongue and cutlass now? [*He looks at him steadily;* AUGUSTIN *throws down the cutlass and turns away*] Old man, your wife is dead, and sorry make you mad. Go on the morne and count the birds like Ragamin, and play bamboo under the wood-trees for you' goat. Is land you know, old man, you don't know sea, you know the fifteen kind of grass this island have, land hard under a old man foot and hard on old woman body, but this sea is no cemetery for old men; go on the morne behind the presbytery, watch goat, talk with priest, and drink your white rum after the night come. When we come back we will talk of this sea.

AUGUSTIN

Afa and Augustin will bring Hounakin fish, and bread, and vegetable from Gacia garden, and when Noel come will drink red rum and talk. Because you woman dead you want to drown?

HOUNAKIN

[*Touching* AFA'*s hand*] Cousin, it cold, it always making cold.

AUGUSTIN

[*Kneeling near the canoe*] So what you have, old man, you cannot sleep? Sixty years you work in cane field, rice swamp, Barnard land, your two eyes come so small you cannot see. Old man, the sun come up, and sea have work. Let Afa and Augustin go to work for you . . . [HOUNAKIN *puts* AFA'*s hand away. It is now broad daylight.* HOUNAKIN *gets up from the narrow canoe, takes his things and is leaving, the two fishermen watching him, when, thinking again, he turns to them*]

HOUNAKIN

[*Resting his pail*] Cousin, I must give my heart tongue, or it will break. You know the stories Rama did tell you Augustin . . . ?

AFA

And me, when I was small . . . *messieurs, crik-crack* . . .

AUGUSTIN

I never forget, papa . . . that is long time . . .

HOUNAKIN

[*Walks painfully nearer*] Like you say, Afa, and my son Augustin, God bless.

[*He sits*]

Since she dead it have two days I only counting birds,
And even bird have woman, fisherman know;
I know where they fly making nest for wind by Pointe,
But they still screaming: "Rama dead, old man, old man,
    Rama dead."
To dead; what is to dead? not dead I fraid . . .
For old man that is nothing, wind.
But when one woman you loving fifty years,
That time they dead, it don't like they should have bird,
And bread to eat, a house, and dog to feed.
It is to take a net in you hand to catch the wind,
To beat head on a stone, to take sand in you' hand,
And that is it, *compère*, that is it true,
When Rama dead I cry after the dog tired.

AFA

All Dauphin know that old man . . . Sit down . . . You
want some bread?

HOUNAKIN

Non, non, merci, I only keep you back . . . The sun break
long . . .

AUGUSTIN

Today Afa can wait . . .

HOUNAKIN

Don't worry, you will not see this old man so again, only,
a man must talk, old man talk to the wind or man go mad
. . . [AFA *offers him bread*] I have no heart to eat. I old,
old, more old than Dauphin self. Rama and I see when

66

didn't have no Dauphin, only cane, and a green river by the
canes. We come here first.

AFA

Sit down, papa. [*He gives him some bread, the old man
smiles, then puts it in his shirt.* AUGUSTIN *gives him a cigarette, which he holds absently, unlit, while talking. He has
sat down*]

HOUNAKIN

When Rama dying she did want more medicine,
You know we could not beg, but then I beg
For one whole year, then she catch sick again.
And Rama say no medicine we must not beg.
I did not want to beg and Rama die.
The first time I did beg you was last night.
To work. I cannot beg or bend down to make garden.
I know have friend, but friend and pride is different . . .
Is just a work to feed a old man and the dog . . .

AFA

Sea will go down, *vieux corps*, come with your cousin.

HOUNAKIN

Non. You must go. The sea rough for two weeks. If Afa not
go, will have no more fish again. *Non* . . . God is
good . . .

AUGUSTIN

A *canot* not no coffin for a old man.
Tonight we will drunk and joke in Samuel café,
Bringing back good fish, and for Rama grave

67

A white shell is at the bottom of the sea . . .
And when sea calm, and God not so vex . . .

HOUNAKIN

Paix, paix garçon . . . An old man must have strength.
Nobody know God height. and nobody know the deep the
    green sea is,
Wind does not pull bird where wind want, look there!
It looking like somebody shaking this basin of the world,
And making waves where man and boats is drowning. Is
    God.
All that; but me self, Hounakin, what I do wrong?
I poor is not my fault. I sin, I make sorry, did have pride,
But that gone now. Me one alone, who don't know night
    from day,
My two eyes come so small. I kneel on my two knees,
I say, when Rama coughing all this time,
God you is old man like me, you put me here, I pray, I
    work,
I never steal when my belly full of wind . . .
I sin, I make confession, is the same.
I work, make absolution is the same.
I love, I have no child, and is the same,
Is seventy years they giving man to live, even old coolie,
But I spit in the face of nothing.
You break your back for seventy cane reap times
And then is ashes. A man cannot fight nothing, after all.
But wind is coming high, Houna must go.

AUGUSTIN

Papa . . . do not do nothing to yourself . . .

68

HOUNAKIN

Houna will not kill himself. This sea have many navels, many waves, and I did feel to die in Dauphin sea, so I could born. *Au'voir* cousin . . . [*Goes off*]

AUGUSTIN

Another day, old man, when sea is calm and wind is soft . . .

AFA

He cannot hear . . .

AUGUSTIN

And a white shell for Rama is in the ground . . .

AFA

[*Starting to push canoe*] *À nous, à nous, compère,* sea going down, and the sun hot . . . [*They start to haul the canoe*] *Plus fort. Poussez! Poussez!* [*The old man can be seen a little above them, watching them at work*] Mind the sail, Agos, mind the sail! [*The old man remains watching them dazedly, and waves a worn, tired hand, then goes off as the lights fade into evening and the almost blinding twilight. The sunset is reddening as the villagers of Dauphin can be heard singing; they are mostly women and a boy, dressed poorly, with bare feet and baskets for the catch, and they come from different parts of the beach, with the young French priest, Father Lavoisier*]

CHORUS OF DAUPHIN WOMEN

[*Singing*]

La mer pwend Bolo qui 'tait si bwave, oy!

Si la mer pwend mwen 'ous pas kai save, oy!
Ba-bye doux-doux, ba-bye, mwen ka aller,
Si mwen mort jourd'hui, pas pleurez!

(The sea took Bolo who was so brave, oh!
When the sea takes me you will not know, oh!
Farewell, darling, farewell, I must go,
If I should die today, don't cry, don't cry.)

'Ous ni un 'tit mouton blanc tout moune save, woy!
Pas quittez-li pleurer pis 'ous pas brave, woy!
Mwen pas ni l'argent pous ba 'ous m'a ni l'or
Pwend vieux canot mwen l'heure mwen mort.

(You have a little white sheep everyone knows, oh!
Don't let it bleat because you aren't brave, oh!
I have no money to give you, I have no gold,
When I die, take this canoe that is too old.)

Ba-bye doux-doux, ba-bye, priez-Dieu pour mwen,
Prie-Dieu pour toute nomme qui ni vent en la main.
Ba-bye doux-doux, ba-bye, l'heure pêcheur mort
Pas ni malheur, pas ni la mer encore.

(Farewell, my love, farewell, pray for me,
Pray for all men with only the wind in their hands
Farewell, my love, farewell, when fishermen die
There is no more bad luck and no more sea.)

A WOMAN

The *canot* is there, where Afa and Augustin?

70

ANOTHER

I tell you I see them go up by Houna house. Looking for the old man—

FIRST WOMAN

[*Pointing left*] Look. They coming.

> [AFA *and* AUGUSTIN *come in.* AUGUSTIN *is worried and carries a white shell in his hand.* AFA *carries a pail of fish, cord, etc. They see the small group, and wait*]

AFA

Is true, then, priest?

AUGUSTIN

We come back long, before the sun lying down, his house is close. Is true this thing we hear? We stand up by his house and hear this singing. If is fish you want, don't have no fish.

AFA

When it happen, *père?*

P. LAVOISIER

[*Urges the boy forward gently*] Jules, go and talk to your uncle, Augustin.

AFA

Oui! Is better than any priest saying *bettise* about God for me to fling salt water in his face!

AUGUSTIN

Afa, you mad?

71

JULES

What to say, *père?*

AUGUSTIN

Jules, my nephew, tell us what you see?

AFA

Tell us what you see, *garçon,* and you put God in it, I cut
your throat!

JULES

I find him by . . . I was looking for whelks with Baptiste,
M'sieu Afa, I find him by the rocks by Pointe . . . Baptiste
was frighten and take run . . . I run and call the *père* . . .

AUGUSTIN

[*Breaks down*]

I cannot take no more, I cannot take no more . . .

[*A woman goes over to him*]

P. LAVOISIER

Augustin, my son, let the wind come, sea come, let the hurricane blow. It will blow the sand from the heart of many a
man and change this world . . .

AUGUSTIN

[*To the woman*] He was mad, he had nothing, he beg us
this morning to take him, but we go . . . Afa have fish for
him, half a bonito, and I have this shell . . .

JULES

Is fall he fall down from the high rocks by Point Side. His face mash up; I wasn't fraid, he fall and the sea take him . . .

WOMAN

True. When you old you don't have nothing.

AUGUSTIN

He didn't have nobody or nothing.

P. LAVOISIER

He had God . . .

AFA

God! [*He turns and empties the fish pail on the sand*] That is God! A big fish eating small ones. And the sea, that thing there, not a priest white, pale like a shark belly we must feed until we dead, not no young Frenchman lock up in a church don't know coolie man dying because he will not beg! [*The women break up and retreat before him*] *Sacrés cooyons! Sacrés jamettes saintes!* All you can do is what, sing way! way! Hounakin dead and Bolo dead, is all mouth! mouth! [*He turns and tears a scapular from his neck and hurls it to the ground*] *Mi! Mi!* Pick it up, *père,* is not ours. This scapular not Dauphin own! Dauphin people build the church and pray and feed you, not their own people, and look at Dauphin! *Gadez lui!* Look at it! You see? Poverty, dirty woman, dirty children, where all the prayers? Where all the money a man should have and friends when his skin old? Dirt and prayers is Dauphin life, in Dauphin, in Canaries, Micoud. Where they have priest is poverty. [*The people leave*] Go home! *Allez-la-caille 'ous!* . . . *Allez!* Idiots, *garces!* . . . [*The priest, Augustin and Jules remain*]

AUGUSTIN

Don't mind him, Father. He must curse or he will cry.

P. LAVOISIER

We are all trying, Afa. I am young here. We must help one another. [*The priest picks up the scapular*] You must take it back . . .

AFA

Why for?

P. LAVOISIER

Afa, leave what you cannot understand to me . . .

AFA

Move in front of me.

AUGUSTIN

Give it to me, *père*. He will take it tomorrow.

AFA

Like dog!

P. LAVOISIER

You fishermen are a hard race. You think we cannot help you? You are wrong. It is a sacred profession, Afa, the first

saints followed your profession, Saint Pierre, Saint Jean.
They were hard-headed men too . . .

AFA

Eh, heh . . . priest, I have nothing against you, leave me
alone. You curse me, I curse you, all right?

P. LAVOISIER

I will pray for you . . .

AFA

Pray for the dead.

P. LAVOISIER

Augustin has your scapular. [*Exit*]

> [AUGUSTIN *and the boy* JULES *wait, watching* AFA *fix some
> twine, pause, then fix it again.* JULES *tugs at* AUGUSTIN'S
> *shoulder and whispers.* AUGUSTIN *walks over to* AFA, *who
> is staring, mumbling, out to sea*]

AUGUSTIN

Tomorrow again?

AFA

Unless you going to church. Because one old man dead,
the sea will stop?

AUGUSTIN

Quant-même we don't have to wait for no old man . . .
We start too late this morning . . .

AFA

À quatre heures juste . . . Four o'clock.

[JULES *tugs at* AUGUSTIN's *shoulder*]

AUGUSTIN

Afa (*whose back is still turned to them*), you always saying
in Samuel café we want another man is not too heavy to
bail, and haul up the *nasse,* this one here want to go with
us tomorrow. His father was Habal, you used to work sea
first in Habal boat, when you did half the old he is . . .

AFA

Half the boat is yours.

AUGUSTIN

Captaine, he have to sit in your half too when fishpots in.

AFA

[*Turning*] Tell him if he know what it have in this trade,
in this season any day is to die. And tell the boy it make
you sour and old and good for nothing standing on two feet
when forty years you have. Ask him why he not going to
Castries to learn mechanic or work in canes. Ask him if he
remember Habal, and then Bolo. If he say yes, tell him he
must brave like Hounakin, from young he is. Brave like
Habal to fight sea at Dauphin. This piece of coast is make
for men like that. Tell him Afa do it for his father sake.
Although Augustin say he have no gratitude . . . Four
o'clock . . .

[JULES *runs over and hugs* AFA. AFA *gives* AUGUSTIN *the*
fish, and the boy and AUGUSTIN *go out.* AFA *sits on the*

*stage, exactly as he did before, wrapping some twine
and smoking. The sound of the* WOMEN *singing faintly
throughout.* GACIA *the fisherman comes in, his straw hat
flapping, quite drunk. He sees* AFA, *then rests his hat
down on the ground. He has a pint bottle of white rum,
which he rests carefully against the canoe*]

GACIA

[*Spelling lettering of the canoe*] Our Daily Bread . . .
Our Daily Bread. [*Holds up the bottle*] You want one?

AFA

[*Takes a drink*] Merci, boug. [*Rests his hand on* GACIA's
shoulder] Merci. [*Offers a cigarette*] Cigarette?

GACIA

[*Shakes his head, mouth full*] Woy! Whole day! . . . Tonight they have his wake. You going?

[*A* WOMAN's VOICE *calling "Gacia, Gacia, oy!"*]

AFA

Your woman calling you.

GACIA

[*Shaking his shoulders in disgust*] Quittez-lui crier! Is
woman work to cry. When you woman Anna coming back?

AFA

I have no woman. I cannot love woman. [*Takes another
drink*] My head is full of madness. I make my heart hard
long. From the first time it break. Nothing breaking it
again. [*Passes back the bottle*]

GACIA

A man cannot live so. Man not a rock.

AFA

I don't know, *boug*. They had a time was like Augustin could cry in front of woman. No more, *jamais encore, garçon*. [*Looks to the sea*] *Belle jour demain.*

GACIA

Peut-être. I finish with the sea . . .

AFA

You always finish with the sea. But you and I, *compère*, we cannot finish.

GACIA

If you leave women I can leave the sea . . . Why you must curse the priest?

AFA

I was vex . . . It mean nothing.

GACIA

Alors, the old man die. He kill himself they say. Sorry can make old man mad. You catch anything?

AFA

One bonito. And a shell.

GACIA

Eh-heh . . .

AFA

In the evening when sun go down behind Maria Island we come back and don't see the old man. We walk up all the beach where we leave him, and go up to his *ajoupa* . . . It have white sea all day around Maingot, but no good fish . . .

GACIA

Ay, *boug!*

AFA

And Augustin have half a bonito for the old man, and so we go up the *ajoupa* on the hill by Dauphin side. And he not there, is only his woman grave. And the garden dead, the old corn dying standing up and the yellow dog is hungry. And Augustin wrap the fish, half a bonito, and put it on top the house and a banana leaf to mark it. And coming down the hill just now we hear the woman singing, and I look at Agos and he look at me afraid. And we meet Debel drunk looking for us and Debel say this morning he see him sitting on the sand and counting bird. [*Takes a drink*] And this afternoon Debel come back, was to catch crab, and he is not there, only the wood-trees and the sand blowing . . . And Debel say he look for him and meet a old man was driving goat from dry grass, and say he see him climbing on the high rocks by where they have the statue of Sainte Vierge . . . And this afternoon they had a boy was fishing for whelks under La Vierge by Maingot side, and see this thing, and the boy turn it over on the sand with his foot, and when they look is him. And the fish on top his house is rotten, faster than old man is dead . . .

79

WOMAN'S VOICE

Gacia! Gacia!

GACIA

Alors?

AFA

[*Looking to sea*] Last year Annelles, and Bolo, and this year
Hounakin . . . And one day, tomorrow, you Gacia, and
me . . . And Augustin . . . And we have only this shell
for his old woman is in the *cimetière* behind the church,
where Fond River coming down by the canes and making
one with the sea at Dauphin . . .

GACIA

Sun going down . . .

AFA

The sea too . . .

GACIA

Tomorrow again. *Un autre demain* . . .

[WOMAN'S VOICE *calling "Gacia, Gacia"*]

AFA

[*Rising*] Your woman crying for you . . . Help me with
this sail. *Aidez, aidez-moi avec voile-là.*

[*They furl the sail*]

NIGHT

Ti-Jean and His Brothers

FOR PETER WALCOTT

CHARACTERS

CRICKET

FROG

FIREFLY

BIRD

GROS JEAN

MI-JEAN

TI-JEAN

MOTHER

BOLOM

{
OLD MAN, or PAPA BOIS

PLANTER

DEVIL
}

(*Ti-Jean and His Brothers* was first performed at the Little Carib Theatre, Port of Spain, Trinidad, in 1958 with the following cast:

William Webb as GROS JEAN; Horace James as MI-JEAN; Freddie Kissoon as TI-JEAN; Jean Herbert and Veronica Jenkin, both of whom played the MOTHER; Russell Winston as BOLOM; Errol Jones as the DEVIL; and Bertrand Henry as FROG. The musicians were John Henderson, Gene Lawrence, Colin Laird and Michael Warren. The play was revived by the Trinidad Theatre Workshop in June 1970 at the Town Hall, Port of Spain, with original music by Andre Tanker and with the following cast: Adele Bynoe as CRICKET, Hamilton Parris as FROG, Roslyn Rappaport as BIRD, Claude Reid as GROS JEAN, Stanley Marshall as MI-JEAN, Belinda Barnes as THE BOLOM, Ellsworth Primus as TI-JEAN, Ormine Wright as the MOTHER and Albert LeVeau as PAPA BOIS, the PLANTER, and the DEVIL.)

Prologue

Evening. Rain. The heights of a forest. A CRICKET, a FROG, a FIREFLY, a BIRD. Left, a hut with bare table, an empty bowl, stools. The MOTHER waiting.

FROG

Greek-croak, Greek-croak.

CRICKET

Greek-croak, Greek-croak.

[*The others join*]

FROG

[*Sneezing*]

Aeschylus me!
All that rain and no moon tonight.

CRICKET

The moon always there even fighting the rain
Creek-crak, it is cold, but the moon always there
And Ti-Jean in the moon just like the story.

[BIRD *passes*]

85

CRICKET

Before you fly home, listen,
The cricket cracking a story
A story about the moon.

FROG

If you look in the moon,
Though no moon is here tonight,
There is a man, no, a boy,
Bent by a weight of faggots
He carried on his shoulder,
A small dog trotting with him.
That is Ti-Jean the hunter,
He got the heap of sticks
From the old man of the forest
They calling Papa Bois,
Because he beat the devil,
God put him in that height
To be the sun's right hand
And light the evil dark,
But as the bird so ignorant
I will start the tale truly.

[*Music*]

Well, one time it had a mother,
That mother had three sons.
The first son was Gros Jean.
That son he was the biggest,
His arm was hard as iron,
But he was very stupid.

86

[Enter GROS JEAN, *a bundle of faggots in one hand, an axe over his shoulder, moving in an exaggerated march to music. The creatures laugh]*

FROG

The name of the second son,
They was calling him Mi-Jean,
In size, the second biggest,
So only half as stupid; now,
He was a fisherman, but
Always studying book, and
What a fisherman; for
When he going and fish,
Always forgetting the bait,
So between de bait and debate . . .

CRICKET

Mi boug qui tait cooyon!
(Look man who was a fool!)

[Roll of drums. Comic quatro, martial]

[Enter MI-JEAN *from the opposite side, carrying a book in one hand and a fishing net over his shoulder. Half-way across the stage he flings the net casually, still reading]*

BIRD

How poor their mother was?

[Sad music on flute]

FROG

Oh that was poverty, bird!
Old hands dried up like claws

87

Heaping old sticks on sticks,
too weak to protect her nest.
Look, the four of that family

[*Light shows the hut*]

Lived in a little house,
Made up of wood and thatch,
On the forehead of the mountain,
Where night and day was rain,
Mist, cloud white as cotton
Caught in the dripping branches;
Where sometimes it was so cold
The frog would stop its singing

[*The* FROG *stops. Five beats. Resumes*]

The cricket would stop rattling
And the wandering firefly
That lights the tired woodsman
Home through the raining trees
Could not strike a damp light
To star the wanderer home!

[*The music stops. The brothers* GROS JEAN *and* MI-JEAN
*put their arms around each other, and to heavy drums
tramp home*]

CRICKET
I damned sorry for that mother.

FROG
Aie, cricket, you croak the truth!
The life of an old woman
With her husband cold in earth,

Where the bamboo leaves lie lightly,
And smell of mouldering flesh,
How well I know that story!
Near where the mother was,
Across the wet and melancholy
Mountain where her hut was, O God,
The Devil used to live!

> [*Crash of cymbals. Shrieks, thunder. The animals cower
> as the* DEVIL *with his troop of fiends, the Werewolf, the
> Diablesse, the* BOLOM, *somersault and dance across the
> stage. The sky is red*]

DEVIL

Bai Diable-là manger un 'ti mamaille!
(Give the Devil a child for dinner!)

DEVILS

Un, deux, trois 'ti mamaille!
(One, two, three little children!)

> [*They whirl around the stage leaping, chanting, then as
> suddenly go off*]

BIRD

Wow!
Were they frightened of him?

FROG

If they were frightened?
They were frightened of his skin,
Powdery as leprosy,
Like the pock-marked moon,

Afraid of his dead eye,
That had no fire in it . . .

CRICKET
Of the terrible thunder
In his wood-shaking throat!

[*Roar of devils off-stage*]

FROG
Just hear them in the hut . . .

[*Sad flute, as the light comes up on the three sons around the knees of the old woman*]

GROS JEAN
One time again it have nothing to eat,
But one dry bread to break;
I went out to chop some wood
To make a nice fire,
But the wood was too damp,
So I didn't use the axe
As I didn't want it to get wet;
If it get wet it get rusty.

MI-JEAN
Sense!
I went out to do fishing
For crayfish by the cold stones,
In the cold spring in the ferns,
But when I get there so,
I find I lack bait,

[*Rising solemnly*]

Now for man to catch fish,
That man must have bait,
But the best bait is fish,
Yet I cannot catch no fish
Without I first have bait,
As the best bait for fish
Is to catch fish with fish,
So I . . .

GROS JEAN

Mi-Jean is a fool,
Reading too much damn book.

MOTHER

My sons, do not quarrel,
Here all of us are starving,
While the planter is eating
From plates painted golden,
Forks with silver tongues,
The brown flesh of birds,
And the white flesh of fish,
What did you do today,
My last son Ti-Jean?

TI-JEAN

Maman, m'a fait un rien.
(Mama, I didn't do a thing.)

GROS JEAN

We do all the damned work.

91

MI-JEAN

We do all the damn thinking.

GROS JEAN

And he sits there like a prince.

MI-JEAN

As useless as a bone.

GROS JEAN AND MI-JEAN

[*Jeering*]

Maman, m'a fait un rien!
Maman, m'a fait un rien!

MOTHER

Wait, and God will send us something.

GROS JEAN

God forget where he put us.

MI-JEAN

God too irresponsible.

MOTHER

Children!

[*Weird music. The* BOLOM *or Foetus rolls in unheard, somersaults around the hut, then waits. Sound of wind, rain, shriek of insects*]

Children, listen,

There is something listening
Outside of the door!

GROS JEAN

I don't hear nothing.

MI-JEAN

I hear only the rain,
Falling hard on the leaves,
And the wind down the throat
Of the gorge with the spring,
The crickets and the bull-frog,
And maybe one frightened bird.

MOTHER

[*Standing*]

I tell you there is something
Outside of the door,
I tell you from experience
I know when evil comes.
It is not the wind, listen!

[*The* BOLOM *imitates a child crying*]

MI-JEAN

A young child out in the forest.

GROS JEAN

Looking for its mother.

MOTHER

The Devil has sent us

93

Another of his angels!
I prayed to God all day,
While I scrubbed the hut bare,
On the knuckles of my knees
All day in the hungry house;
Now God has sent me evil,
Who can understand it?
Death, death is coming nearer.

GROS JEAN

Line the step with fine sand
To keep the evil out!

MI-JEAN

Turn over, Mother, the hem of your skirt!

GROS JEAN AND MI-JEAN

Let two of our fingers form in one crucifix!

[TI-JEAN *steps outside*]

MOTHER

Spirit that is outside,
With the voice of a child
Crying out in the rain,
What do you want from the poor?

[TI-JEAN *searches carefully*]

BOLOM

I have a message for a woman with three sons.

MOTHER

Child of the Devil, what is your message?

BOLOM

Send the first of your sons outside for it,
They must die in that order. And let the youngest
Return into the hut.

[TI-JEAN *steps back into the hut*]

MOTHER

We can hear you in the wind,
What do you want of me?

[*A weird light shows the* BOLOM. *Shrieks*]

ALL

Where are you? Where is it?
Hit it! There! Where is it?

BOLOM

[*Leaping, hiding*]

Here, in the bowl!
Here, sitting on a stool!
Here, turning in a cup!
Here, crawling up your skirt!

MOTHER

I have done you no harm, child.

BOLOM

A woman did me harm,
Called herself mother,
The fear of her hatred
A cord round my throat!

95

MOTHER

[Turning, searching]

Look, perhaps it is luckiest
Never to be born,
To the horror of this life
Crowded with shadows,
Never to have known
That the sun will go out,
The green leaf rust,
The strong tree be stricken
And the roaring spring quail;
Peace to you, unborn,
You can find comfort here.
Let a mother touch you,
For the sake of her kind.

BOLOM

[Shrieks, dancing back]

Whatever flesh touches me,
Withers me into mortality;
Not till your sons die, Mother,
Shall this shape feel this life.

GROS JEAN

[Seizes axe]

Kill it, then, kill it.

MI-JEAN

Curse it back to the womb.

DEMON'S VOICE

Faire ca mwen di ous!
(Do what I commanded!)

BOLOM

I hear the voice of my master.

DEMON'S VOICE

Bolom, faire tout ça mwen dire ous!
(Child, do all that I ordered you!)

BOLOM

Listen, creature of gentleness,
Old tree face marked with scars,
And the wounds of bearing children,
Whom the earth womb will swallow,
This is the shriek
Of a child which was strangled,
Who never saw the earth light
Through the hinge of the womb,
Strangled by a woman,
Who hated my birth,
Twisted out of shape,
Deformed past recognition,
Tell me then, Mother,
Would you care to see it?

[BOLOM *moves out of the light, shrieking*]

GROS JEAN

Let us see you!

97

MOTHER

The sight of such horror, though you are brave,
Would turn you to stone, my strong son, Gros Jean.

MI-JEAN

Let us reason with you.

MOTHER

My son, the thing may be a ball of moving fire,
A white horse in the leaves, or a clothful of skin,
Found under a tree, you cannot explain that!

BOLOM

Save your understanding for the living,
Save your pity for the dead,
I am neither living nor dead,
A puny body, a misshapen head.

MOTHER

What does your white master
The Devil want from us?

BOLOM

The house looks warm, old woman,
Love keeps the house warm,
From the cold wind and cold rain;
Though you bar up the door,
I can enter the house.

[*Thunder*]

MOTHER

Enter! You are welcome.

[*She flings open the door*]

GROS JEAN AND MI-JEAN

Shut the door, shut the door!

[*Crash of cymbals. The* BOLOM *rolls in a blue light towards the hut, then enters; all freeze in fear*]

BOLOM

The Devil my master
Who owns half the world,
In the kingdom of night,
Has done all that is evil
Butchered thousands in war,
Whispered his diseases
In the ears of great statesmen,
Invented human justice,
Made anger, pride, jealousy,
And weakened prayer;
Still cannot enjoy
Those vices he created.
He is dying to be human.
So he sends you this challenge!
To all three of your sons,
He says through my voice,
That if anyone on earth

[DEVILS' VOICES *chanting*]

Anyone human
Can make him feel anger,
Rage, and human weakness,

99

He will reward them,
He will fill that bowl,
With a shower of sovereigns,
You shall never more know hunger,
But fulfillment, wealth, peace.

[*Increased drum roll to climax*]

But if any of your sons
Fails to give him these feelings,
For he never was human,
Then his flesh shall be eaten,
For he is weary of the flesh
Of the fowls of the air,
And the fishes in the sea,
But whichever of your sons
Is brave enough to do this,
Then that one shall inherit
The wealth of my prince.
And once they are dead, woman,
I too shall feel life!

[*Exit*]

DEVILS' VOICES OFF
Bai Diable-là manger un 'ti mamaille,
Un, deux, trois 'ti mamaille!
Bai Diable-là manger un 'ti mamaille,
Un,
      deux,
            trois . . .
(Give the Devil a child for dinner,

One, two, three little children!
Give the Devil a child for dinner,
One,
    two,
        three . . .)

FADEOUT

Scene One

Daybreak. The hut. The MOTHER and her sons asleep. GROS JEAN rises, packs a bundle. His MOTHER stirs and watches. He opens the door.

MOTHER

You will leave me just so,
My eldest son?

GROS JEAN

Is best you didn't know.

MOTHER

Woman life is so. Watching and losing.

GROS JEAN

Maman, the time obliged to come I was to leave the house, go down the tall forest, come out on the high road, and find what is man work. Is big man I reach now, not no little boy again. Look, feel this arm, but to split trees is nothing. I have an arm of iron, and have nothing I fraid.

MOTHER

The arm which digs a grave

Is the strongest arm of all.
Your grandfather, your father,
Their muscles like brown rivers
Rolling over rocks.
Now, they bury in small grass,
Just the jaws of the ant
Stronger than them now.

GROS JEAN

I not even fraid that. You see,
Is best you still was sleeping?
I don't want to wake my brothers.
Ti-Jean love me and will frighten.
Mi-Jean will argue and make me remain.
The sun tapping me on my shoulder.

MOTHER

When you go down the tall forest, Gros Jean,
Praise God who make all things; ask direction
Of the bird, and the insects, imitate them;
But be careful of the hidden nets of the devil,
Beware of a wise man called Father of the Forest,
The Devil can hide in several features,
A woman, a white gentleman, even a bishop.
Strength, *ça pas tout*, there is patience besides;
There always is something stronger than you.
If is not man, animal, is God or demon.

GROS JEAN

Maman, I know all that already.

MOTHER

Then God bless you, Gros Jean.

GROS JEAN

The world not the same it was in your time,
Tell my brothers I gone. A man have to go.

> [*Marches from hut*]

> [*Martial flute, quatro, drum*]

GROS JEAN

> [*Sings*]

There's a time for every man
To leave his mother and father
To leave everybody he know
And march to the grave he one!

> [*Enter the animals, hopping around him*]

So the time has come for me
To leave me mother and father
To add my force to the world
And go to the grave me one!

> [*The FROG is in his path. He aims a kick*]

Get out of my way, you slimy bastard! How God could
make such things? Jump out under my foot, cricket, you
know you have no bones! *Gibier! Gibier, montrez-moi
sortir!* Bird-o, bird-o, show me a good short-cut, be quick!

> [*Suddenly the BIRD, CRICKET and the FROG all scurry
> shrieking, croaking. The OLD MAN enters limping and
> rests a bundle of faggots down. GROS JEAN watches. The*

104

OLD MAN *lifts a corner of his robe to scratch a cloven,*
hairy hoof. GROS JEAN *emerges*]

GROS JEAN

Bon jour, vieux papa.

OLD MAN

Bon matin, Gros Jean.

GROS JEAN

What you have with your foot?

OLD MAN

Fleas, fleas, boy.

[*Covers it quickly*]

GROS JEAN

Is man I am now. Chiggers in your flesh?
Is man I am, papa, and looking for success.

OLD MAN

The flesh of the earth is rotting. Worms.

GROS JEAN

Which way, papa?

OLD MAN

I cannot tell you the way to success;
I can only show you, Gros Jean,
One path through the forest.

GROS JEAN

I have no time to waste. I have an arm of iron,

It have nothing, I fraid, man, beast, or beast-man,
And more quick I get what I want, more better.

OLD MAN

I think strength should have patience. Look at me today.
I was a strong woodman, now I burn coals,
I'm as weak as ashes. And nearly deaf. Come nearer.

GROS JEAN

[*Advances calmly*]

What you would say is the quickest way?

OLD MAN

The quickest way to what?

GROS JEAN

To what counts in this world.

OLD MAN

What counts in this world is money and power.

GROS JEAN

I have an arm of iron, only money I missing.

OLD MAN

Then I can't advise you.

GROS JEAN

You old and you have experience.
So don't be selfish with it.

Or you know what I'll do.

[*Grabs him, hurls him down, axe uplifted*]

Chop you and bury you in the bamboo leaves!

OLD MAN

With your arm of iron, the first thing to kill is wisdom?

GROS JEAN

That's right, papa.

OLD MAN

Well, the Devil always wants help.

GROS JEAN

The Devil boasts that he never get vex.

OLD MAN

[*Rising*]

Easy, easy son, I'll help you if you wait,
Just let me adjust the edge of my skirt.
Well, I was coming through the forest now
And I passed by the white spring, and I saw
Some poor souls going to work for the white planter.
He'll work you like the devil, but that's what you want,
You and your impatience and arm cast in iron,
So turn to the right, go through the bamboo forest,
Over the black rocks, then the forest will open,
And you will see the sky, below that a valley,
And smoke, and a white house that is empty,

The old fellow is hiring harvesters today.
Remember an iron arm may rust, flesh is deciduous.
There's your short-cut, Gros Jean, make the most of it.

GROS JEAN
Next time don't be so selfish.

[*Exit* GROS JEAN, *marching*]

OLD MAN

[*Sings, gathering bundle*]

Who is the man who can speak to the strong?
Where is the fool who can talk to the wise?
Men who are dead now have learnt this long,
Bitter is wisdom that fails when it tries.

[*To the audience*] Ah well, there's wood to cut, fires to light, smoke to wrinkle an old man's eyes, and a shrivelling skin to keep warm. There went the spirit of war: an iron arm and a clear explanation, and might is still right, thank God, for God is the stronger. But get old father forest from the path of the fable, for there's wood to cut, a nest of twittering beaks to feed with world-eating worms. Oh, oh, oh.

[*The creatures creep after him timidly*]

For they all eat each other, and that's natural law,
So remember the old man in the middle of the forest.

[*He turns suddenly. Then hobbles after them*]

Eat and eat one another! It's another day. Ha, ha! Wah! Wah!

[*They flee. He goes out*]

GROS JEAN

[*In another part of the wood*] I have an arm of iron, and that's true, but I here since the last two days working for this damn white man, and I don't give a damn if he watching me. You know what I doing here with this bag and this piece of stick? Well, I go tell you. While I smoke a pipe. Let me just sit down, and I won't lose my patience. [*He sits on a log*] Well, you remember how I leave home, and then bounce up this old man who put me on to a work? Remember what the old son of a leaf-gathering beggar said? He said that working for the Devil was the shortest way to success. Well, I walked up through the bush then I come onto a large field. Estate-like, you know. Sugar, tobacco, and a hell of a big white house where they say the Devil lives. Ay-ay.

So two next black fellers bring me up to him. Big white man, his hand cold as an axe blade and his mind twice as sharp. So he say, "Gros Jean, we has a deal to make, right?" So I say, "Sure, boss!" He say the one that get the other one vex, the one who show the first sign of anger will be eaten rrruuunnnhhh, just like that, right? You think I stupid? I strong, I have some sense and my name not Gros Jean for nothing. That was two days ago. Well, Jesus, a man ain't rest since then! The first job I had, I had was to stand up in a sugar-cane field and count all the leaves of the cane. That take me up till four o'clock. I count all the leaves and then divide by the number of stalks. I must tell you there had times when I was getting vex but the old iron arm fix me, because there is patience in strength. The Devil ain't say anything. About seven o'clock, he tell me to go and catch about seventy fireflies. Well, you must try and catch fireflies! Is not easy. Had a time when I do so once, one whap with the hand! thinking was a bunch but was nothing, only stars! So in the middle of all that, this man come up to me and say, what's the matter, Joe, he always like he don't know my name, but I is me, Gros Jean, the strongest! And if you ain't know my name, you best don't call me nothing. Say, "What's matter, Mac? You vex or sumpin?" So I say, "No, I ain't vex!" Well, is two days now, and I ain't get a cent. I so tired I giddy. But I giving the old iron arm a rest from cramp, and breaking a little smoke. After all! If was only sensible work, if a man could get the work that suit him, cotton or sugar or something important! Plus he getting eighty-five per cent of the profit? Shucks, man, that ain't fair. Besides I could just bust his face, you know. But me mother ain't bring me up so. After all, man, after all, a man have to rest man. Shime!

[*Enter* DEVIL. *masked as a* PLANTER]

PLANTER
Well, how's it progressing, Joe, tired?

GROS JEAN
From where you was and now you come you hear me say I fagged? [*Slowly*] And Gros Jean is the name, boss.

PLANTER
Tobacco break? Whistle's blown past lunch, boy.

GROS JEAN

I taking a five here, chief. Black people have to rest too, and once I rest, chief, I do more work than most, right?

PLANTER

That's right, Mac.

GROS JEAN

[*Gritting his teeth*] Gros Jean . . . Gros . . . Jean . . . chief . . . !

PLANTER

You sound a bit annoyed to me.

GROS JEAN

[*With a painful, fixed grin from now on*] Have your fun. I know I ain't nobody yet, chief, but an old man tell me to have patience. And I ain't let you down yet, chief, hasn't I?

PLANTER

That's right, Gros Chien, Gros Jean, Gros Jean, sorry. Can't tell one face from the next out here. How's the work then? [*Pacing up and down*]

GROS JEAN

Chief, why you don't take a rest too somewhat? You have all this land, all this big house and so forth, people working for you as if is ants self, but is only work, work, work in your mind, ent you has enough?

PLANTER

[*Looking at his watch*] Other people want what I have,

Charley, and other people have more. Can't help myself, Joe, it's some sort of disease, and it spreads right down to the common man.

GROS JEAN

I not no common man, boss. People going hear about Gros Jean. Because I come from that mountain forest, don't mean I can't come like you, or because I black. One day all this could be mine!

PLANTER

Yes, yes. Well anyway, Horace, time is flying, and I want these leaves checked, counted, filed and classified by weight and texture and then stacked . . . What's the matter, Francis?

GROS JEAN

[*To audience*] You see how he provoking me, you don't think I should curse his . . . [*Turns, bites hard on pipe, grinning*] Look, I haven't let you down yet, boss, have I? I mean to say I take two three hours to catch your goat you send me to catch. I mean not so? Wait, chief, wait, listen . . . I ain't vex, boss. Ha-ha!

PLANTER

Sit down, Joe, relax, you can't take it with you, they say, only time is money, and the heights that great men reached etc., and genius is ninety per cent perspiration and so forth . . . So, sit down, waste time, but I thought you were in a hurry . . . Henry.

GROS JEAN

Boss. [*Smiling*] You really impatianate, yes. Ha-ha! I mean
I don't follow you, chief. After I count and carry all the
cane leaves for you, ain't I, and look—when the wind blow
them wrong side I ain't say nothing, and I'm smiling ain't
I? [*Relaxes his expression, then resumes*] I'm smiling because I got confidence in the old iron arm, ain't it? And if
I do it and have time to spare is the work and pay that
matter, and is all you worried about, *big shot!* Ain't it?
Excuse me, I mean to say, I'm smiling ain't I?

PLANTER

Sorry, sorry, Gros Jean, sometimes we people in charge of
industry forget that you people aren't machines. I mean
people like you, Hubert . . .

[GROS JEAN *is about to sit*]

GROS JEAN

[*Rising*] Gros Jean, chief, Gros Jean . . . Ha-ha!

PLANTER

Gros Jean, very well . . . [*Pause*] Have your smoke. [*Pause*]
Plenty of time. It might rain, people may be stealing from
me now. The market is unsteady this year. [*Pause*] But
we're human. [*Pause*] You don't know what it means to
work hard, to have to employ hundreds of people. [*Embracing him*] You're worth more to me, Benton, than fifty men.
So you should smoke, after all. [*Pause*] And such a pleasant
disposition, always smiling. [*Pause, steps back*] Just like a
skull. [*Long pause*] But remember, Mervin, I'd like you to

try and finish this, you see I have a contract and the harder
you work the more I . . .

GROS JEAN

[*Exploding, smashing pipe in anger*] Jesus Christ what this
damn country coming to a man cyant even get a goddamned
smoke? [*He tries to grin*] I ent vex, I ent vex, chief. Joke,
joke, boss . . .

EXPLOSION

[*When the smoke clears, the* DEVIL, *his* PLANTER's *mask
removed, is sitting on the log, calmly nibbling the flesh
from a bone*]

DEVILS' VOICES OFF

Bai Diable-là manger un 'ti mamaille
   Un!
(Give the Devil a child for dinner
   One! . . .)

BLACKOUT

Scene Two

Music. Dawn. The forest. A cross marked "Gros Jean." The creatures foraging. Enter MI-JEAN walking fast and reading, a net slung over his shoulder)

BIRD

[*To flute*]

Mi-Jean, Mi-Jean, *bon jour*, M'sieu Mi-Jean.

[*The creatures dance*]

MI-JEAN

[*Closes the book*]

Bird, you disturbing me!
Too much whistling without sense,
Is animal you are, so please know your place.

CRICKET

Where you going, Mi-Jean?

MI-JEAN

[*To the audience*]

But see my cross, *oui*, ay-ay!

Since from what time cricket
Does ask big man their business?

FROG

You going to join your brother?
You are a man's size now.

MI-JEAN

[*Again to the audience*]

Well, confusion on earth, frog could talk!
Gros Jean was one man, I is a next. Frog,
You ever study your face in
The mirror of a pool?

BIRD

Mi-Jean, Mi-Jean,
Your brother is a little heap
Of white under the bamboo leaves,
Every morning the black beetles
More serious than a hundred priests,
Frowning like fifty undertakers
Come and bear a piece away
To build a chapel from his bones. Look, look!

[BIRD *shows the cross.* MI-JEAN *kneels and peers through his spectacles*]

CRICKET

Every morning I sit here,
And see the relics of success,
An arm of iron turned to rust,
Not strong enough to stir the dirt.

FROG

Gros Jean was strong, but had no sense.

MI-JEAN

[*Rising and dusting his clothes*]

He had the sin called over-confidence!
Listen, I . . .

BIRD

Run, run, Papa Bois, Papa Bois . . .

[*All run off*]

OLD MAN

Bon jour, Mi-Jean, Mi-Jean, *le philosophe.*

MI-JEAN

[*To the audience*]

When my mother told me goodbye in tears,
She said, no one can know what the Devil wears.

[*To the* OLD MAN]

Bon jour, Papa Bois, how come you know my name?

OLD MAN

Who in the heights, in any small hut hidden in the ferns,
where the trees are always weeping, or any two men are
ploughing on a wet day, wrapped in old cloaks, or down
in the villages among the smoke and rum, has not heard of
Mi-Jean the jurist, and the gift of his tongue, his prowess
in argument, Mi-Jean, the *avocat,* the fisherman, the liti-

117

gant? Come, come, sir, don't be modest! I've been sitting there on the cold, crusty log, rough as the armoured bark of a frog, waiting to exchange knowledge with you. Ah, your brother's grave! How simple he was! Well, I'm half-blind, but I see you have one virtue more than your brother, fear. Nothing lives longer than brute strength, sir, except it is human cowardice. Come nearer, come nearer, and tell us why you left home? Sit down, you're among equals.

MI-JEAN

I good just where I am.
I on my way to the sea
To become a rich captain,
The land work too hard.
Then to become a lawyer.

OLD MAN

[*Softly singing*]

On land on sea no man is free,
All meet death, the enemy. I see,
Hence the net, the net and the book.

MI-JEAN

What?

OLD MAN

I say hence the book,
Hence the net, and the book.

MI-JEAN

Ça c'est hence? (What is "hence"?)

OLD MAN

Same as whereas, and hereunto affixed.
These are terms used in tautology and law.

MI-JEAN

[*Nodding blankly. Pause. Then*:]

I see you have a cow-foot. Ain't that so?

OLD MAN

Yes, yes. A cow's foot. You have an eye for detail!
Born with it, actually. Source of embarrassment.
Would you like some tobacco? What are you reading?

MI-JEAN

[*Opens the book*]

This book have every knowledge it have;
I checking up on man with cow-foot, boss,
In the section call religion, and tropical superstition.
Bos . . . *Bovis* . . . Cow . . . foot . . . foot, boss? Boss
   foot? *Bovis?*

OLD MAN

Outside in the world they are wiser now, Mi-Jean;
They don't believe in evil or the prevalence of devils,
Believe me, philosopher, nobody listens to old men;

Sit down next to me and have a bit of tobacco.
And since you need knowledge, I'll give you advice . .

MI-JEAN

[*Still reading*]

I don't smoke and I don't drink,
I keep my head clear, and advice,
I don't need none, but will listen.

[*Shuts the book*]

This book is Latin mainly.
It have *bos,* meaning cow,
and *pes,* meaning foot,
Boss' foot, *bospes,* cow-heel perhaps,
It have plenty recipe
But it don't give the source! [*Sighs loudly*] So!
Yes, apart from wisdom, I have no vices.

OLD MAN

Life without sin. How about women?

MI-JEAN

The downfall of man! I don't care for women,
Women don't have no brain. Their foot just like yours.

OLD MAN

You believe in the Devil?
Oh, why don't you sit nearer,
Haven't you ever seen a cow-heel before?

MI-JEAN

Not under a skirt, no. [*Sighs loudly*] Yes!
I believe in the Devil, yes,
Or so my mother make me,
And is either that, papa,
Or not believe in God.
And when I meet this devil,
Whatever shape he taking,
And I know he is not you,
Since he would never expose
His identity so early,
I will do all that he commands,
But you know how I will beat him,

     [*Sits near the* OLD MAN]

With silence, and a smile.

     [*He smiles*]

Too besides when I meet him,
I will know if God exist,
We calling that in philosophy

     [*Checks in the book*]

We calling that in big knowledge,
Ah, polarities of belief,
When the existence of one object
Compels that of the other,
Bon Dieu, what terms, what terms!

     [*Sighs loudly, rests the book down*]

Yes. Silence shall be my defence.

[*He sings "The Song of Silence"*]

I

Within this book of wisdom
Hear what the wise man say:
The man who is wise is dumb
And lives another day,
You cannot beat the system
Debate is just a hook,
Open your mouth, de bait in!
And is you they going to juck

CHORUS

So when things dark, go blind
When nothing left, go deaf
When the blows come, be dumb
And hum, hum.

II

In Chapter Five from para-
Graph three, page 79,
This book opines how Socra-
Tes would have been better off blind.
God gave him eyes like all of we,
But he, he had to look.
The next thing, friends, was jail, *oui!*
Hemlock and him lock up!

CHORUS

So when things dark, go blind, etc.

III

The third set of instruction
This self-said book declares
Is that the wise man's function
Is how to shut his ears
Against riot and ruction
That try to climb upstairs.
If you can hear, don't listen!
If you can see, don't look!
If you must talk, be quiet!
Or your mouth will dig your grave.

> [*While he sings his song, the* OLD MAN *goes behind a grove of bamboo, leisurely removes his robe and his mask, under which is the mask of the* DEVIL; *then he changes into the mask and clothes of the* PLANTER.]

PLANTER

[*He sits on the log, legs crossed, smiling throughout the scene*] Ah, finished all the work I gave you, Mi-Jean?

[MI-JEAN *nods*]

And menial work didn't bore you, a thinker?

[MI-JEAN *nods*]

You're not one for small-talk, are you?

[MI-JEAN *nods*]

Did you catch the wild goat?

[MI-JEAN *nods yes*]

Frisky little bugger, wasn't he? Yes, sir, that's one hell of a goat. Some kid, what? Clever, however. How many canes were there on the estate?

[MI-JEAN *uses ten fingers repeatedly*]

Don't waste words, eh? All right, all right. Look, you don't mind a little chat while we work, do you? A bit of a gaff lightens labour. Good Lord, man, you've been here for over two days and haven't had the common decency to even pass the time of day. Where did you get your reputation as a bush lawyer, I mean it's only manners, blast it.

[MI-JEAN *cocks his head at the* PLANTER]

Oh, don't flatter yourself, young man, I'm not annoyed. It takes two to make a quarrel. Shut up, by all means. [*Rises*] Now, before it gets dark, I want you to come up to the house, check and polish the silver, rearrange my library and . . .

[*The goat bleats.* MI-JEAN *frowns*]

Aha, looks like the old goat's broken loose again, son. Better drop what you're not doing and catch it before it's dark.

[MI-JEAN *rises rapidly, runs off, returns*]

Ah, now you're smiling again, fixed him this time, haven't you?

[*The goat bleats*]

Not quite, cunning animal, that goat, couldn't have tied him.

[MI-JEAN *dashes out, annoyed, returns*]

Fast worker!

[*The goat bleats*]

Look, before you dash off, I'd like to say here and now . . .

[*The goat bleating as* MI-JEAN, *mumbling, smiling, points off*]

that I do admire your cheery persistence, your resigned non-chalance, so let me demonstrate something. There's a special kind of knot, and there's an end to that. Hence you take the rope thus, and whereas the goat being hereto affixed to the . . .

[*Goat bleating,* MI-JEAN *raging inside*]

but if that doesn't fix him, then my recommendation is . . .

MI-JEAN

Look!

PLANTER

Yes?

MI-JEAN

I think I know what I'm doing . . . sir . . .

PLANTER

[*Above the sound of bleating*] Oh, sure, sure. But I was simply trying to explain just to help you out, that . . . [*Goat bleats*] . . . You see? He's gone off again! Just a little more patience . . . [MI-JEAN *is about to run off*] It's simply a question of how you tie this knot, don't you see? [MI-JEAN, *collecting himself, nods, then tiredly smiles*] I mean, I've seen dumber men, not you, fail at this knot you know, it's just a matter of know-how, not really knowledge, just plain skill . . . [MI-JEAN *nodding, nodding*] You look the kind of fellow who doesn't mind a bit of expert advice. [*Goat bleats furiously*] And you'd better hurry up before it gets dark. Wait, remember how to tie the knot.

MI-JEAN

[*Under control, nods*] Yes, I remember. [*Runs off, crosses the stage several times in a chase*]

PLANTER

[*Walks up and down in a rage*] Well, what the hell, I thought I had him there, he's no fool, that's certain, for the Devil comes in through apertures. He doesn't know right from wrong, and he's not interested. The only entrance I could have got through his mouth, I tried to leave ajar, but the fool bolted it completely. There he goes chasing the bloody goat like a simpleton, and not even shouting at it. Good old Master Speak No Evil. I hope he breaks his God-supported neck, the dummy! [*He sits*] Here comes the comedy again, an eloquent goat and a tongueless biped!

[*The goat cavorts across and around the stage to merry music, with* MI-JEAN *behind him waving a rope and the net.* MI-JEAN *collapses*]

PLANTER

Tough life, eh?

[MI-JEAN *groans, nodding*]

Don't let it get you down.

126

[*Goat bleats*]

MI-JEAN

That goat certainly making a plethora of cacophony.

PLANTER

It's only a poor animal, in its own rut.

MI-JEAN

[*Smiling*] Men are lustiferous animals also, but at least they have souls.

PLANTER

Ah, the philosopher! The contemplative! An opinion at last! A man is no better than an animal. The one with two legs makes more noise and that makes him believe he can think. It is talk that makes men think they have souls. There's no difference, only in degree. No animal, but man, dear boy, savours such a variety of vices. He knows no season for lust, he is a kneeling hypocrite who on four legs, like a penitent capriped, prays to his maker, but is calculating the next vice. That's my case!

MI-JEAN

Nonsensical verbiage! *Bettise!*

PLANTER

It's not, you know, and you're getting annoyed.

MI-JEAN

[*Shakes his head*] You can't get me into no argument! I

have brains, but won't talk. [*Long pause*] All I say is that man is divine!

PLANTER

You're more intelligent than the goat, you think?

MI-JEAN

I not arguing! Anything you want.

PLANTER

[*Rises*] Honestly, I'd like to hear what you think. You're the kind of chap I like to talk to. Your brother was a sort of politician, but you're a thinker.

[MI-JEAN, *rising, is about to lecture. The goat bleats*]

Steady-on. For all we know, that may be poetry. Which Greek scholar contends in his theory of metempsychosis that the souls of men may return into animals?

MI-JEAN

I never study Greek, but I . . . [*Goat bleats.* MI-JEAN *pauses*] I was saying that I never study no Greek but I'd . . . [*Goat bleats*] It getting on like to have sense, eh?

PLANTER

Why not?

MI-JEAN

Listen, I ent mind doing what you proposed, anything physical, because that's ostentatious, but when you start theorising that there's an equality of importance in the creatures of this earth, when you animadvertently imbue mere animals with an animus or soul, I have to call you a crooked-minded pantheist . . . [*Goat bleats, sounding like "Hear, hear!"*] Oh, shut up, you can't hear two people talking? No, I'm not vexed, you know, but . . . [*Goat bleats*]

PLANTER

[*Advancing towards him*] Your argument interests me. It's nice to see ideas getting you excited. But logically now. The goat, I contend, may be a genius in its own right. For all we know, this may be the supreme goat, the apogee of capripeds, the voice of human tragedy, the Greek . . .

MI-JEAN

Exaggerated hypothesis! Unsubstantiated!

PLANTER

Since the goat is mine, and if you allow me, for argument's sake, to pursue my premise, then if you get vexed at the goat, who represents my view, then you are vexed with me, and the contract must be fulfilled.

MI-JEAN

I don't mind talking to you, but don't insult me, telling me a goat have more sense than I, than me. Than both of we!

PLANTER

[*Embracing him*] Descendant of the ape, how eloquent you have become! How assured in logic! How marvellous in invention! And yet, poor shaving monkey, the animal in you is still in evidence, that goat . . . [*Goat sustains its bleat-ing*]

MI-JEAN

Oh, shut you damn mouth, both o'all you! I ain't care who right who wrong! I talking now! What you ever study? I ain't even finish making my points and all two of you interrupting, breach of legal practice! O God, I not vex, I not vex . . .

[PLANTER *removes his mask, and the* DEVIL *advances on* MI-JEAN]

EXPLOSION

BLACKOUT

[*The goat bleats once*]

DEVILS' VOICES OFF

Bai Diable-là manger un 'ti mamaille
(Give the Devil a child for dinner)
Un!
(One!)
Deux!
(Two! . . .)

INTERVAL

Scene Three

Dawn. The forest. Two crosses marked "Gros Jean," "Mi-Jean." The OLD MAN sits on the log, the creatures huddle near him. TI-JEAN, MOTHER, in the hut.

DEVILS' VOICES OFF

Bai Diable-là manger un 'ti mamaille,
Un, deux, trois 'ti mamaille!
Bai Diable-là manger un 'ti mamaille,
Un, deux, trois 'ti mamaille.

OLD MAN

Aie! Feed the Devil the third, feed the Devil the third.
Power is knowledge, knowledge is power, and the Devil
devours them on the hour!

DEVILS

Bai Diable-là manger un 'ti mamaille,
Un, deux, trois 'ti mamaille!

OLD MAN

[*To audience*] Well, that's two good meals finished with a

131

calm temper, and if all goes mortally, one more is to come.
[*Shrieks, points to where* TI-JEAN *is consoling his* MOTHER]
Aie, ya, yie, a chicken is to come, a calf, a veal-witted young
man, tender in flesh, soft in the head and bones, tenderer
than old muscle power, and simpler than that net-empty
atheist. For the next dish is man-wit, common sense. But I
can wait, I can wait, gathering damp rotting faggots, aie!

MOTHER

[*To flute*]

If you leave me, my son,
I have empty hands left,
Nothing to grieve for.
You are hardly a man,
A stalk, bending in wind
With no will of its own,
Never proven your self
In battle or in wisdom,
I have kept you to my breast,
As the last of my chickens,
Not to feed the blind jaws
Of the carnivorous grave.

TI-JEAN

You have told me yourself
Our lives are not ours,
That no one's life is theirs
Husband or wife,
Father or son,
That our life is God's own.

MOTHER

You are hard, hard, Ti-Jean,
O what can I tell you?
I have never learnt enough.

TI-JEAN

You have taught me this strength,
To do whatever we will
And love God is enough.

MOTHER

I feel I shall never see you again.

TI-JEAN

To return what we love is our glory, our pain.

OLD MAN

Oh, enough of these sentiments, I'm hungry, and I'm cold!

TI-JEAN

Now pray for me, *maman,*
The sun is in the leaves.

MOTHER

The first of my children
Never asked for my strength,
The second of my children
Thought little of my knowledge,
The last of my sons, now,
Kneels down at my feet,
Instinct be your shield,

It is wiser than reason,
Conscience be your cause
And plain sense your sword.

[*The* BOLOM *rolls towards the hut. Drums*]

BOLOM

Old tree shaken of fruit,
This green one must die.

MOTHER

Aie, I hear it, I hear it,
The cry of the unborn!
But then have I not given
Birth and death to the dead?

[*The* BOLOM *dances off, shrieking.* TI-JEAN *rises*]

Oh, Ti-Jean, you are so small,
So small. [*Exit*]

TI-JEAN

Yes, I small, *maman*, I small,
And I never learn from book,
But, like the small boy, David.

[*Sings*]

I go bring down, bring down Goliath,
Bring down below.
Bring down, bring down Goliath,
Bring down below.

[*He enters the forest*]

Ti-Jean and His Brothers

TI-JEAN

Ah, *bon matin, compère Crapaud,*
Still in your dressing-gown?

FROG

Ti-Jean, like your brothers you're making fun of me.

TI-JEAN

Why should I laugh at the frog and his fine bass voice?

FROG

You wouldn't call me handsome, would you?

TI-JEAN

[*Kneels among the* CREATURES]

Oh, I don't know, you have your own beauty.
Like the castanet music of the cricket over there.

CRICKET

Crak, crak. Now say something nice to the firefly.

FIREFLY

How can he? I don't look so hot in the daytime.

TI-JEAN

But I have often mistaken you at night for a star.

[*Rises*]

Now friends, which way is shortest to the Devil's estate?

135

FROG

Beware of an old man whose name is wordly wisdom.

FIREFLY

With a pile of sticks on his back.

CRICKET

. . . and a foot cloven like a beast.

TI-JEAN

If he is an old man, and mortal,
He will judge everything on earth
By his own sad experience.
God bless you, small things.
It's a hard life you have,
Living in the forest.

FIREFLY

God preserve you for that.
Bird, take the tree and cry
If the old man comes through
That grove of dry bamboo.

[*Bird flies off*]

CRICKET

Crashing through the thicket
With the cleft hoof of a beast.

FIREFLY

For though we eat each other,
I can't tempt that frog too close,

136

And we never see each other for dinner,
We do not do it from evil.

FROG

True. Is a long time I never eat a firefly.

FIREFLY

Watch it, watch it, brother,
You don't want heartburn, do you?

TI-JEAN

No, it is not from evil.
What are these crosses?

CRICKET

Nothing. Do not look, Ti-Jean.
Why must you fight the Devil?

TI-JEAN

To know evil early, life will be simpler.

FROG

Not so, Ti-Jean, not so. Go back.

[TI-JEAN *goes to the crosses, weeps*]

BIRD

Weep-weep-weep-weep-quick,
The old man is coming, quick.

FROG

If you need us, call us, brother, but

You understand we must move.

[TI-JEAN *stands over the crosses*]

OLD MAN

Ah, good morning, youngster! It's a damp, mournful walk through the forest, isn't it, and only the cheep of a bird to warm one. Makes old bones creak. Now it's drizzling. Damn it.

TI-JEAN

Bon jou, vieux cor', I find the world pleasant in the early light.

OLD MAN

They say, the people of the forest, when the sun and rain contend for mastery, they say that the Devil is beating his wife. Know what I say? I say it brings rheumatism, I don't believe in the Devil. Eighty-eight years, and never seen his face.

TI-JEAN

Could you, being behind it?

OLD MAN

Eh? Eh? I'm deaf, come nearer. Come here and shelter. Good. Some people find me ugly, monstrous ugly. Even the small insects sometimes. The snake moves from me, and this makes me sad. I was a woodsman once, but look now. I burn wood into ashes. Let me sit on this log awhile. Tobacco?

138

TI-JEAN

No, thanks, sir.

OLD MAN

Tell me, boy, is your father living? Or your mother perhaps? You look frail as an orphan.

TI-JEAN

I think nothing dies. My brothers are dead but they live in the memory of my mother.

OLD MAN

You're very young, boy, to be talking so subtly. So you lost two brothers?

TI-JEAN

I said I had brothers, I never said how many. May I see that foot, father?

OLD MAN

In a while, in a while. No, I saw you looking at the two graves, so I presumed there were two. There were two, weren't there? Ah well, none can escape that evil that men call death.

TI-JEAN

Whatever God made, we must consider blessed. I'm going to look at your foot.

OLD MAN

Hold on, son. Whatever God made, we must consider
blessed? Like the death of your mother?

TI-JEAN

Like the death of my mother.

OLD MAN

Like the vileness of the frog?

TI-JEAN

[*Advancing*] Like the vileness of the frog.

OLD MAN

Like the froth of the constrictor?

TI-JEAN

Like the froth of the constrictor. [*He is above the* OLD MAN]

OLD MAN

Like the cloven cow's foot under an old man's skirt?

[TI-JEAN *sweeps up the skirt, then drops it*]

What did you hope to find, but an old man's weary feet?
You're a forward little fool! Now, do you want some advice?
Tell me how you'll face the Devil, and I'll give you advice.

TI-JEAN

O help me, my brothers, help me to win.

[*He retreats to the crosses*]

140

OLD MAN

Getting frightened, aren't you? Don't be a coward, son.
I gather twigs all day, in the darkness of the forest,
And never feared man nor beast these eighty-eight years.
I think you owe me some sort of apology.

> [*The* BIRD *runs out and begins to peck at the rope, untying the faggots with his beak. The* OLD MAN *jumps up, enraged*]

Leave that alone, you damned . . .

TI-JEAN

I'll help you, father.

> [*Instead, he loosens the bundle*]

OLD MAN

I'll kill that bird. Why did you loosen my sticks?
Haven't you any respect for the weariness of the old?
You've had your little prank, now help me collect them.
If you had a father you'd know what hard work was,
In the dark of the forest, lighting damp faggots . . .

> [TI-JEAN *pretends to be assisting the* OLD MAN, *but carefully he lifts his skirt and sees that below the sackcloth robe he has a forked tail*]

TI-JEAN

My mother always told me, my spirits were too merry,
Now, here we are, old father, all in one rotten bundle.

OLD MAN

What's come over you, you were frightened a while back?

TI-JEAŃ

Which way to the Devil? Oh, you've never seen him.
Tell me, does the Devil wear a hard, stiff tail?

OLD MAN

How would I know. [*Feels his rear, realises*] Mm. Well, you
go through that track, and you'll find a short-cut through
the bamboo. It's a wet, leaf-rotting path, then you come to
the springs of sulphur, where the damned souls are cook-
ing . . .

TI-JEAN

You sure you not lying?

OLD MAN

It's too early in the morning to answer shallow questions,
That's a fine hat you're wearing, so I'll bid you goodbye.

[TI-JEAN *lifts up a stick*]

TI-JEAN

Not until I know who you are, papa!
Look, I'm in a great hurry, or I'll brain you with this;
If evil exists, let it come forward.
Human, or beast, let me see it plain.

[*The stage darkens. Drums. The* OLD MAN *rises*]

OLD MAN

Very well then, look!

[*He unmasks: the* DEVIL'*s face. Howls, cymbals clash*]

DEVIL

Had you not gotten me, fool,

142

Just a trifle angry,
I might have played the Old Man
In fairness to our bargain,
But this is no play, son.
For here is the Devil,
You asked for him early,
Impatient as the young.
Now remember our bargain,
The one who wastes his temper,
Will be eaten! Remember that!
Now, you will work!

TI-JEAN

Cover your face, the wrinkled face of wisdom,
Twisted with memory of human pain,
Is easier to bear; this is like looking
At the blinding gaze of God.

DEVIL

[*Replacing* OLD MAN's *mask, and changing*]

It is hard to distinguish us,
Combat to fair combat, then I cover my face.
And the sun comes out of the rain, and the clouds.
Now these are the conditions, and the work you must do.

TI-JEAN

Wait, old man, if is anything stupid,
I don't have your patience, so you wasting time.

OLD MAN

Then you must pay the penalty.

These are your orders:
I have an ass of a goat
That will not stay tied.
I want you to catch it
Tonight before sundown.
Over hill and valley
Wherever it gallops.
Then tie it good and hard.
And if it escapes
You must catch it again
As often as it gets loose
You try as many times.
If you should lose your temper . . .

TI-JEAN

Where the hell is this goat?

OLD MAN

Over there by the . . . wait.
The fool has run off.
He won't last very long.

[*Exit* TI-JEAN. *The* OLD MAN *sits down, rocking back and
forth with laughter.* TI-JEAN *runs back*]

OLD MAN

Finished already?

TI-JEAN

That's right. Anything else?

OLD MAN

Ahm. Yes, yes, yes. Best I've seen, though.

Now I want you to go down to the edge of the cane
field . . .

[*The goat bleats*]

Looks like you didn't tie him?

TI-JEAN

I tied the damned thing up.
Something is wrong here.
I tied the thing up properly.

[*The* OLD MAN *laughs.* TI-JEAN *runs off. The* OLD MAN
dances with joy. Goat bleats, then stops suddenly. TI-
JEAN *returns with something wrapped in a banana leaf
and sits down quietly. The* OLD MAN *watches him. Pause.
No bleat*]

OLD MAN

What's that in your hands?

TI-JEAN

[*Proffers the leaf*]

Goat seed.

[*The goat bleats girlishly*]

OLD MAN

His voice is changing.
I don't get you. Goat-seed?

TI-JEAN

I tied the damn thing.
Then made it a eunuch.

[*The goat bleats weakly*]

Sounds much nicer.

OLD MAN

You er . . . fixed my one goat?
Then you must have been angry.

TI-JEAN

No, I just couldn't see myself
Chasing the damned thing all night.
And anyhow, where I tied it,
She'll never move again.

OLD MAN

[*Walking around stage*]

You sit there calm as hell
And tell me you er . . . altered Emilia?

TI-JEAN

Funny goat, with a girl's name,
It's there by the plantain tree,
Just by the stones.

OLD MAN

Boy, you have a hell of a nerve.

TI-JEAN

It look like you vex.

OLD MAN

Angry? I'm not angry. I'm not vexed at all.

146

You see? Look! I'm smiling.
What's an old goat anyhow
Just the only goat I had.
Gave sour milk anyway.

TI-JEAN

[*Rising. Rubbing his hands*]

Fine. Now, what's next on the agenda?

OLD MAN

What? Yes, yes . . . Fixed the goat . . .

TI-JEAN

Now look here, life is . . .

OLD MAN

Enough of your catechism!

TI-JEAN

Temper, temper. Or you might lose something. Now what
    next?

OLD MAN

Now, listen to this, boy.
Go down to the cane-fields
And before the next cloud
Start checking every blade,
Count each leaf on the stalk,
File them away properly
As fast as you can

147

Before the night comes,
Then report back to me.
Well, what are you waiting for?

TI-JEAN

I got a bit tired chasing the goat,
I'm human you know.

OLD MAN

I'm going back to the house,
I'll be back at dawn to check on your progress.

[*Exit*]

TI-JEAN

[*Goes to the edge of the cane-field*]

Count all the canes, what a waste of time!

[*Cups his hands*]

Hey, all you niggers sweating there in the canes!
Hey, all you people working hard in the fields!

VOICES

[*Far off*]

'Ayti? What happen? What you calling us for?

TI-JEAN

You are poor damned souls working for the Devil?

VOICES

Yes! Yes! What you want?

TI-JEAN

Listen, I'm the new foreman! Listen to this:
The Devil say you must burn everything, now.
Burn the cane, burn the cotton! Burn everything now!

VOICES

Burn everything now? Okay, boss!

[*Drums. Cries. Caneburners' chorus*]

TI-JEAN

The man say Burn, burn, burn de cane!

CHORUS

Burn, burn, burn de cane!

TI-JEAN

You tired work for de man in vain!

CHORUS

Burn, burn, burn de cane!

[*Exeunt*]

[*The Frog enters*]

FROG

[*Sings*]

And all night the night burned
Turning on its spit,
Until in the valley, the grid
Of the canefield glowed like coals,
When the devil, as lit as the dawn returned,

Dead drunk, and singing his song of lost souls.

[*Enter* DEVIL, *drunk, with a bottle, singing*]

DEVIL

Down deep in hell, where it black like ink,
Where de oil does boil and the sulphur stink,
It ain't have no ice, no refrigerator
If you want water, and you ask the waiter,
He go bring brimstone with a saltpetre chaser,
While de devils bawling.

[*He is carrying the* OLD MAN's *mask. Now he puts it on*]
Oh, if only the little creatures of this world could understand, but they have no evil in them . . . so how the hell
can they? [*The* CRICKET *passes*] Cricket, cricket, it's the old
man.

CRICKET

Crek, crek, boo!

CHORUS

Fire one! Fire one
Till the place burn down,
Fire one! Fire one.

DEVIL

[*Flings the mask away*]

I'll be what I am, so to hell with you. I'll be what I am. I
drink, and I drink, and I feel nothing. Oh, I lack heart to

enjoy the brevity of the world! [*The* FIREFLY *passes, dancing*] Get out of my way, you burning backside, I'm the prince of obscurity and I won't brook interruption! Trying to mislead me, because I been drinking. Behave, behave. That youngster is having terrible effect on me. Since he came to the estate, I've felt like a fool. First time in me life too. Look, just a while ago I nearly got angry at an insect that's just a half-arsed imitation of a star. It's wonderful! An insect brushes my dragonish hand, and my scales tighten with fear. Delightful! So this is what it means! I'm drunk, and hungry. [*The* FROG, *his eyes gleaming, hops across his path*] O God, O God, a monster! Jesus, help! Now that for one second was the knowledge of death. O Christ, how weary it is to be immortal. [*Sits down on log*] Another drink for confidence.

[*Sings*]

When I was the Son of the Morning,
When I was the Prince of Light.

[*He picks up the mask*]

Oh, to hell with that! You lose a job, you lose a job.
tion. Yet we were one light once up there, the old m;
I, till even today some can't tell us apart.

[*He holds the mask up. Sings*]

And so I fell for forty days,
Passing the stars in the endless pit.

Come here, frog, I'll give you a blessing. [*The* FROG *hops back, hissing*] Why do you spit at me? Oh, nobody loves me, nobody loves me. No children of my own, no worries of my own. To hell with . . . [*Stands*] To hell with every stinking one of you, fish, flesh, fowl . . . I had the only love of God once [*Sits*] but I lost that, I lost even that.

[*Sings*]

Leaning, leaning,
Leaning on the everlasting arms . . .

To hell with dependence and the second-lieutenancy! I had a host of burnished helmets once, and a forest of soldiery waited on my cough, on my very belch. Firefly, firefly, you have a bit of hell behind you, so light me home. [*Roars at the* CREATURES] Get out, get out, all of you . . . Oh, and yet this is fine, this is what they must call despondency, weakness. It's strange, but suddenly the world has got bright, I can see ahead of me and yet I hope to die. I can make out the leaves, and . . . wait, the boy's coming. Back into the Planter. [*Wears the* PLANTER's *mask*]

TI-JEAN

[*Enters, also with a bottle*] Oh, it's you, you're back late. Had a good dinner?

DEVIL

You nearly scared me. How long you been hiding there?

TI-JEAN

Oh, I just came through. Drunk as a fish.

152

DEVIL

Finished the work?

TI-JEAN

Yes, sir. All you told me. Cleaned the silver, made up the fifty rooms, skinned and ate curried goat for supper, and I had quite a bit of the wine.

DEVIL

Somehow I like you, little man. You have courage. Your brothers had it too, but you are somehow different. Curried goat? . . .

TI-JEAN

They began by doing what you suggested. Dangerous. So naturally when the whole thing tired them, they got angry with themselves. The one way to annoy you is rank disobedience. Curried goat, yes.

DEVIL

We'll discuss all that in the morning. I'm a little drunk, and I am particularly tired. A nice bathtub of coals, and a pair of cool sheets, and sleep. You win for tonight. Tomorrow I'll think of something. Show me the way to go home.

TI-JEAN

[*His arms around the* DEVIL.]

Oh, show me the way to go home,
I'm tired and I want to go to bed,
I had a little drink half an hour ago . . .

153

DEVIL

[*Removing his arm*] Wait a minute, wait a minute . . . I
don't smell liquor on you. What were you drinking?

TI-JEAN

Wine, wine. You know, suspicion will be the end of you.
That's why you don't have friends.

DEVIL

You have a fine brain to be drunk. Listen, I'll help you.
You must have a vice, just whisper it in my ear and I won't
tell the old fellow with the big notebook.

TI-JEAN

[*Holds up bottle*] This is my weakness. Got another drink
in there?

DEVIL

[*Passing the bottle*] This is powerful stuff, friend, liquid
brimstone. May I call you friend?

TI-JEAN

You may, you may. I have pity for all power. That's why I
love the old man with the windy beard. He never wastes it.
He could finish you off, like that . . .

DEVIL

Let's not argue religion, son. Politics and religion . . .
You know, I'll confess to you. You nearly had me vexed
several times today.

TI-JEAN

How did my two brothers taste?

DEVIL

Oh, let's forget it! Tonight we're all friends. It gets dull in that big house. Sometimes I wish I couldn't have everything I wanted. He spoiled me, you know, when I was his bright, starry lieutenant. Gave me everything I desired. I was God's spoiled son. Result: ingratitude. But he had it coming to him. Drink deep, boy, and let's take a rest from argument. Sleep, that's what I want, a nice clean bed. Tired as hell. Tired as hell. And I'm getting what I suspect is a hell of a headache. [*A blaze lightens the wood*] I think I'll be going up to the house. Why don't you come in, it's damp and cold out here. It's got suddenly bright. Is that fire?

TI-JEAN

Looks like fire, yes.

DEVIL

What do you think it is, friend?

TI-JEAN

I think it's your house.

DEVIL

I don't quite understand . . .

TI-JEAN

Sit down. Have a drink. In fact, I'm pretty certain it's your home. I left a few things on fire in it.

DEVIL

It's the only house I had, boy.

TI-JEAN

My mother had three sons, she didn't get vexed. Why not smile and take a drink like a man?

DEVIL

[*Removing the* PLANTER's *mask*]

What the hell do you think I care about your mother? The poor withered fool who thinks it's holy to be poor, who scraped her knees to the knuckle praying to an old beard that's been deaf since noise began? Or your two damned fools of brothers, the man of strength and the rhetorician? Come! Filambo! Azaz! Cacarat! You've burnt property that belongs to me.

[ASSISTANT DEVILS *appear and surround* TI-JEAN]

TI-JEAN

You're not smiling, friend.

DEVIL

Smiling? You expect me to smile? Listen to him! [*The* DEVILS *laugh*] You share my liquor, eat out my 'fridge, treat you like a guest, tell you my troubles. I invite you to my house and you burn it!

TI-JEAN

[*Sings*]

Who with the Devil tries to play fair,

156

Weaves the net of his own despair.
Oh, smile; what's a house between drunkards?

DEVIL

I've been watching you, you little nowhere nigger! You little squirt, you hackneyed cough between two immortalities, who do you think you are? You're dirt, and that's where you'll be when I'm finished with you. Burn my house, my receipts, all my papers, all my bloody triumphs.

TI-JEAN

[*To the* DEVILS]

Does your master sound vexed to you?

DEVIL

Seize him!

[*The* BOLOM *enters and stands between* TI-JEAN *and the* DEVIL]

BOLOM

Master, be fair!

DEVIL

He who would with the devil play fair,
Weaves the net of his own despair.
This shall be a magnificent ending:
A supper cooked by lightning and thunder.

[*Raises fork*]

MOTHER

[In a white light in the hut]

Have mercy on my son,
Protect him from fear,
Protect him from despair,
And if he must die,
Let him die as a man,
Even as your Own Son
Fought the Devil and died.

DEVIL

I never keep bargains. Now, tell me, you little fool, if you
aren't afraid.

TI-JEAN

I'm as scared as Christ.

DEVIL

Burnt my house, poisoned the devotion of my servants,
small things all of them, dependent on me.

TI-JEAN

You must now keep
Your part of the bargain.
You must restore
My brothers to life.

DEVIL

What a waste, you know yourself
I can never be destroyed.

They are dead. Dead, look!

[*The* BROTHERS *pass*]

There are your two brothers,
In the agony where I put them,
One moaning from weakness,
Turning a mill-wheel
For the rest of his life,
The other blind as a bat,
Shrieking in doubt.

[*The two* BROTHERS *pass behind a red curtain of flame*]

TI-JEAN

O God.

DEVIL

[*Laughing*] Seize him! Throw him into the fire.

TI-JEAN

[*With a child's cry*] Mama!

DEVIL

She can't hear you, boy.

TI-JEAN

Well, then, you pay her what you owe me!
I make you laugh, and I make you vex,
That was the bet. You have to play fair.

DEVIL

Who with the devil tries to play fair . . .

TI-JEAN

[*Angrily*] I say you vex and you lose, man! Gimme me money!

DEVIL

Go back, Bolom!

BOLOM

Yes, he seems vexed,
But he shrieked with delight
When a mother strangled me
Before the world light.

DEVIL

Be grateful, you would have amounted to nothing, child, a man. You would have suffered and returned to dirt.

BOLOM

No, I would have known life, rain on my skin, sunlight on my forehead. Master, you have lost. Pay him! Reward him!

DEVIL

For cruelty's sake I could wish you were born. Very well then, Ti-Jean. Look there, towards the hut, what do you see?

TI-JEAN

I see my mother sleeping.

DEVIL

And look down at your feet,
Falling here, like leaves,
What do you see? Filling this vessel?

TI-JEAN

The shower of sovereigns,
Just as you promised me.
But something is wrong.
Since when you play fair?

BOLOM

Look, look, there in the hut,
Look there, Ti-Jean, the walls,
The walls are glowing with gold.
Ti-Jean, you can't see it?
You have won, you have won!

TI-JEAN

It is only the golden
Light of the sun, on
My mother asleep.

[*Light comes up on the hut*]

DEVIL

Not asleep, but dying, Ti-Jean.
But don't blame me for that.

TI-JEAN

Mama!

161

DEVIL

She cannot hear you, child.
Now, can you still sing?

FROG

Sing, Ti-Jean, sing!
Show him you could win!
Show him what a man is!
Sing Ti-Jean . . . Listen,
All around you, nature
Still singing. The frog's
Croak doesn't stop for the dead;
The cricket is still merry,
The bird still plays its flute,
Every dawn, little Ti-Jean . . .

TI-JEAN

[*Sings, at first falteringly*]

To the door of breath you gave the key,
Thank you, Lord,
The door is open, and I step free,
Amen, Lord . . .
Cloud after cloud like a silver stair
My lost ones waiting to greet me there
With their silent faces, and starlit hair
Amen, Lord.

[*Weeps*]

DEVIL

What is this cooling my face, washing it like a

Wind of morning. Tears! Tears! Then is this the
Magnificence I have heard of, of
Man, the chink in his armour, the destruction of the
Self? Is this the strange, strange wonder that is
Sorrow? You have earned your gift, Ti-Jean, ask!

BOLOM

Ask him for my life!
O God, I want all this
To happen to me!

TI-JEAN

Is life you want, child?
You don't see what it bring?

BOLOM

Yes, yes, Ti Jean, life!

TI-JEAN

Don't blame me when you suffering,
When you lose everything,
And when the time come
To put two cold coins
On your eyes. Sir, can you give him life.

DEVIL

Just look!

BOLOM

[*Being born*]

I am born, I shall die! I am born, I shall die!

163

O the wonder, and pride of it! I shall be man!
Ti-Jean, my brother!

DEVIL

Farewell, little fool! Come, then,
Stretch your wings and soar, pass over the fields
Like the last shadow of night, imps, devils, bats,
Eazaz, Beelzebub, Cacarat, soar! Quick, quick the sun!
We shall meet again, Ti-Jean. You, and your new brother!
The features will change, but the fight is still on.

[*Exeunt*]

TI-JEAN

Come then, little brother. And you, little creatures.
Ti-Jean must go on. Here's a bundle of sticks that
Old wisdom has forgotten. Together they are strong,
Apart, they are all rotten.
God look after the wise, and look after the strong,
But the fool in his folly will always live long.

[*Sings*]

Sunday morning I went to the chapel
Ring down below!
I met the devil with the book and the Bible.
Ring down below!
Ask him what he will have for dinner.

CHORUS

Ring down below!

TI-JEAN

Cricket leg and a frog with water.

CHORUS

Ring down below!

TI-JEAN

I leaving home and I have one mission!

CHORUS

Ring down below!

TI-JEAN

You come to me by your own decision.

CHORUS

Ring down below!

TI-JEAN

Down in hell you await your vision.

CHORUS

Ring down below!

TI-JEAN

I go bring down, bring down Goliath.

CHORUS

Bring down below!

[*Exeunt. The* CREATURES *gather as before*]

165

And so it was that Ti-Jean, a fool like all heroes, passed through the tangled opinions of this life, loosening the rotting faggots of knowledge from old men to bear them safely on his shoulder, brother met brother on his way, that God made him the clarity of the moon to lighten the doubt of all travellers through the shadowy wood of life. And bird, the rain is over, the moon is rising through the leaves. Messieurs, creek. Crack.

Malcochon
or, The Six in the Rain

*Who is the slayer, who
the victim? Speak!*
Sophocles

CHARACTERS

CONTEUR

OLD MAN

NEPHEW

WOMAN

CHANTAL

HUSBAND

MOUMOU, the deafmute

(*Malcochon* was first performed by the St. Lucia Arts Guild, directed by Roderick Walcott, in 1959. It was revived by the Trinidad Theatre Workshop at the Little Carib Theatre, Port of Spain, with the following cast: Johnny Cayonne as CONTEUR; Fred Hope as the OLD MAN; Claude Reid as the NEPHEW; Lima Hill as the WOMAN; Errol Jones as CHANTAL; Ralph Campbell as the HUSBAND; Geddes Jennings as MOUMOU, the deafmute.)

The Scene

A disused copra house built on a gradual rise between, left, a painted waterfall with rocks; and, right, the edge of a bamboo forest. The shed floor is littered with husks, trash, etc. The musicians play.

CONTEUR

In country rumshops when the flute,
The *shac-shac* and the violon
Mix with the smoke and *malcochon,*
They say, "Sing how Chantal the brute
Took the white planter Regis' life."
And what I tell them is the truth:
Don't believe all you heard or read
Chantal the tiger cannot dead.

> [*Labourers working in the canes: an* OLD MAN, *his* NEPHEW, *another man, and a* WOMAN *carrying water. Drums*]

That day Chantal was stealing wood
Up in the heights above Boissiere.
Three men, one woman was working there
In honest sweat like all men should.
An old man they calling Charlemagne,
His nephew, Sonson, and one Popo,

And Popo woman, Madeleine,
And this is how the history go: . . .

[*They cut the canes, singing. The* OLD MAN *stops. Drums*]

OLD MAN

La pluie! Listen. On the hills there, hear it coming? [*They stop working. Drums increase*] Thunder! And look how dark it get. Is a storm for true, this rain.

WOMAN

Aie! *La pluie, la pluie.* Come go, wooy!

[*They run off. The stage darkens*]

CONTEUR

And up there Chantal chopping wood,
Up in the wet heights by Boissiere
At the crop-over of the year,
Hacking the trees like they had blood.

[*Above the waterfall we see* CHANTAL *working*]

CHANTAL

Même si'ous crier moin Chantal
Nom moin i'c'est Tarzan
Pis moin jeter ti m'ielette crachard
A dans yeux un magistrat
Eur mettaient moin la jaule!
(Even is Chantal you call me
My true name is Tarzan
And just because I hawked and spat
In the eyes of the magistrate
They give me a year in jail.)

Malcochon, or The Six in the Rain

[*Thunder. He stops, gathers bundle, climbs down the rocks. Exit.* OLD MAN, NEPHEW *hurry on*]

OLD MAN

Walk fast! Walk fast! You can't hear that roaring noise like is an animal self crashing in the trees? That's a bad rain coming, and make haste, make haste, nephew, we have to pass Bocage before it reach.

NEPHEW

Don't break your neck for that, Uncle. We had to wait and get pay. And cash don't have no use on a dead man. We'll reach Bocage.

OLD MAN

You have my money, eh? Good. Don't let it get wet. Paper money, it get wet it will get rotten. But make haste, Sonson, make haste! We don't have time to waste.

NEPHEW

Ah! What you so afraid of?

[*Sings*]

Listen, old man,
One, two, three, the white man have plenty,
When thunder roll is a nigger belly empty.

[*Drum roll. Exeunt*]

CONTEUR

[*With dissonant music*]

The rain coming with a sound like sand on dusty leaves,

The leaves rushing in the wind like the hair of a mad-
    woman,
The wind is sweating water, and the river moving faster,
Bamboos bending in the wind and groaning like the posts
That holding up the sky, the sicrier cries through the rain-
    darkness,
The hawk shifts on the branch, shaking knives from its
    wings.

[*Enter the* WIFE, *the* HUSBAND, *in the rain*]

WIFE

What happen to you? What's the matter with you? Let go
my damned hand, I tell you! You want to make me shame
in the middle of the high road? I tell you he give me this
bottle because I do something for him, but your mind so
full of nastiness and mud. Let me go, I tell you. You don't
see the rain coming?

HUSBAND

And a bottle of white rum, a cheap bottle of *malcochon*
that you know which kind of woman does drink, is all that
red nigger overseer could give you? Look at your hair, look
at your face, you like a crazy woman!

WIFE

Is you who crazy! Well then leave me alone, or kill me
then, kill me. Because a man give me a bottle? But I not
standing up in the white rain to talk nastiness with you.

HUSBAND

You not giving me the bottle?

WIFE

I want you to kill me! Kill me, for me to dead laughing!
You not no man, Popo. Follow me, like a dog not even sure
what it smelling.

[*Exit. Thunder*]

HUSBAND

Laugh at me, thunder! Point your hand on me, lightning!
Let the sea show its white teeth and mock me if it want.
But before darkness fall, the rain will have cause to cry.
[*Exit*]

CONTEUR

The rage of the beast is taken for granted,
Man's beauty comes from enduring pain,
The wound shall come when the wound is wanted.
This is the story of six in the rain.

CHANTAL

[*Climbing down rocks*]

Even is Chantal you call me
My name is Tarzan
And just because I hawked and spat
In the eyes of the magistrate

[*Leaping onto ground*]

They putting me in jail.

[*He washes his muddy feet in the basin of the waterfall*]

CHANTAL

Chantal hungry. He hungry after spending three weeks in

the forest, eating bird, small animal and green plantain and sleeping in a trash house in the mountain before the rain come. But blessed are they that hungry for righteousness' sake, as if they catch you stealing one green fig, is praedial larceny! And while like in the old days before God grow a beard they would cut off your right hand for putting food in your mouth, nowadays is just brang! brang! clang! clang! Lock you in the iron bars and the warder swallowing the key. Especially when is Chantal they catch. Give a dog with forty-three convictions a bad name and hang it. Now this is Regis' land. I have nothing against Regis even on Saturday, but I bet if he only catch me here washing my foot like a holy innocent, he will have a dirty mind about me. Must be my face. When I before the bar in petty sessions I try to smile, so, but the scar I get here in a fight once, and the fact that one eye smaller than the next not helping things. Oh, if only I wasn't so ugly, I could sin like a beautiful woman and nobody would hold it against me. Chantal, while you talking you best look for a breadfruit tree to climb and pick your lunch. [*Looks around*] And the magistrates these days so young. The last one I face didn't even look at me. Though maybe he was frighten. He only look up quickly once and say, "Ah yes, Chantal, you come back from vacation, we keep your place for you, nine months' hard labour," like a young wife he just married and that was that. The dance was over and the violin was in the sack. Ah, I see one. With the piece of dry codfish I have and a nice ripe breadfruit, ah . . . [*Stops*] No. I getting to be an old man is best not to steal. If I steal again, what will be the use of spending time in the mountain, in the forest, bawling "Praise be to God"? But is the only thing

I can do well, steal. No. Yes. No. In the old days when I had all my teeth yes, and when the madman Chantal passing through the village and just come out of jail, the children hiding round the corners singing *"Tigre, tigre chou brulé; tigre, tigre chou brulé!"* [*Roars, then laughs*] No. They not feeding me, why they must beat me? My back from the cat with nine tails have more stripe than the tiger. [*A scream. He crosses himself*] God in heaven, maker of rain! Something happen!

[*Exit left*]

MUSICIANS
[*Together*] What happen? What happen?

CONTEUR
[*Holds up hand*] T'à l'heure! Wait!

[*Scream*]

MUSICIANS
[*Drum begins*] Ça y est? Ça y est?

CONTEUR
[*Getting up slowly*] Regis. They kill Regis!
[*Dancing the action*] He lift up the axe.

MUSICIANS
He lift up the axe!

CONTEUR
[*Miming the murder*] And the madness start to dance! Hanche! Is the axe in the wood!

Woy! Woy! They kill Regis!
Woy, Woy! They kill Regis!

[*Drumming and chanting as the* CONTEUR *in a fast dance imitates a hacked man, whirls and drops. Cymbals. Silence.* CHANTAL *enters, his clothes bloody*]

CHANTAL

Bien, bien, bien. [*Sits on rock*] Who care how much it rain? [*Looks at his hands*] Is now I should wash my hands in the cold water. *Bien, bien, bien.* Well, today life finish for me, just so. Like a flash of lightning. Like the signature of a judge. [*Looks at his axe*] Is trees they make you to cut friend. Not the tree that is a man. [*Shudders*] The rain cold. I should wash my hands quick before the poison get down in the bone. [*Goes to waterfall, then stops*] To wash hands is nothing. That is to put poison in this water where beast drink and man drink. Bocage is the source. A child that drink this water with a dead man blood in it, *bien,* is like putting poison in the source itself, for this clear spring bringing water to the villages. *Bon Dieu!* [*Looks up at the rain. The deafmute in loincloth and headcloth comes from the bamboos, carrying a bundle*] Well, friend. We in it now, eh? A dead man in the rain, face down in the mud and the wet leaves, and an idiot with no tongue. Why I come down from the forest at all, rain or no rain? And the bamboo groaning for a dead white man. I know you cannot talk. Nice one for the magistrate. *Bon Dieu!* God, what kind of joke you playing on Chantal? Who will believe me? An old thief? A madman. [*To sky*]

How many times I tell you I change my heart, and is this you send me. [*Thunder*] Ah, shut up! You don't know what to do with this world yourself! What you have there, brother? [*Opens bundle*] Silver spoons. A dead man for a few silver spoons. To hang for that. Come, mongoose, the tiger will help you. We'll chuck him in the ditch by the waterfall. Come. Come with Chantal! O thief without a tongue!

[*Exeunt.* OLD MAN *and* NEPHEW *run into the shed*]

OLD MAN

Cold rain, dead leaves, cold wind, old bones.
Why time can't leave old people alone?

NEPHEW

Ah, hush your mouth and be grateful.

OLD MAN

This morning when we was passing through this short-cut
    self,
I see what look like a nestful of young snakes. Listen,
There have days in this life that look like any other,
But an old man can feel frightened, and not from his ague.
The way the bull-frog croaking with a note like death, and
The angle of a chicken hawk turning on the wind.
Listen, they have something on this place. They have many
    beast
A man cannot see that hiding in a forest. They have bats
    here,
And in this copra trash they could well have snakes. Listen,

In the life of a man, all his darkness, all his sins
Can meet in one place, in the middle of a forest. Like a
  beast. Yes,
Like to meet a beast with no name in the track of the
  bamboo.
I don't like the look of this day from since cock crow.
What noise is that, Nephew?

NEPHEW

What noise, except Bocage?
That waterfall there that is all smoke and white thunder.
The same water that baptising this estate with its name.
Sit down, stop dancing around in this rubbish.

OLD MAN

Bocage, Bocage,
That waterfall, they say it have strange powers,
That it can make some sinners *déparler*,
Talk out their sins for the whole world to know them.
This is Regis land, the planter. Used to husk copra here.
I work here as a young man when your mother was living.
It still smell of oil and trash, and the dung of small animals.
But I am like an old dog pissing on memories.
This was a rich estate once, before rats get the coconuts.
Regis. He living there in the big house, an old white man
  in darkness.
In the old days . . .

NEPHEW

In the old days, in the old days. Damn the old days.
Your mind like a sick crab forever creeping backwards.

In the old days they used to frighten us as children
About Chantal the woodcutter and madman of the forest.
What you doing now? What you looking for, Uncle?

OLD MAN

My money, my money! I lose my money, Sonson!
True, true. As you say, Chantal!

NEPHEW

You give it to me. To put inside my hat.
Look take the damn money and stop troubling me. Blast!
Here! Here! Just now you will ask me for it again.
Take it! [*Offers the money*]

OLD MAN

I didn't remember that I give you to hold it.
It was paper money and a lot. And it get wet,
It get rotten.

NEPHEW

I say take it. I sick of you forever checking on your money.
I sick of other labourers saying how much I make you work,
I don't send you to work. I tired telling you stay home,
Sit in your rocking chair, Uncle, and remember all you
    want.
Remember how your brother kill his wife for your nasti-
    ness,
A man making the beast with the wife of his own brother.
Take the money, take it, and stuff it up your mattress.

OLD MAN

Is not true, is not true. Your father had no right . . .

NEPHEW

Not where he is, dead.
The past don't trouble me. Is your damn babbling!
The past is your responsibility, not mine.
Only remember they hang your brother, my father that was.

OLD MAN

You have the same blood, the madness and the hatred . . .

NEPHEW

And you have plenty you can thank God the Father for.
I buy you a gramophone. It just gathering dust.
I treat you like . . . In fact, man, look.

OLD MAN

The money I am saving is to buy my own house.

NEPHEW

Oh?

OLD MAN

My own dry house, where no wind will come,
Where the rain cannot reach me, and I cannot hear the
    thunder,
A good pitchpine coffin. I cannot live in all this hatred.
Ah God, I could be now in the district of D'Aubaignan
Looking after white sheep on the pastures by the sea
Leaning on an old stick and watching the clouds . . .

NEPHEW

Go then. You don't want the money?

Malcochon, or The Six in the Rain

OLD MAN

Sonson, tell me the truth. You don't want me to die?

NEPHEW

I hungry like hell and is that stupidness you talking?
Die then. Go and die. The house will have more room.

OLD MAN

Wait! Look two strangers coming out of the bush.
The money!

> [*The* NEPHEW *hides the money.* CHANTAL *and* THE MUTE
> *run into a shed*]

OLD MAN

Bon jour, m'sieur. Big rain that, eh? Worse I ever see and I
near seventy years.

> [CHANTAL *picks up the spoons*]

My name is Charlemagne, this is my brother child, Sonson.
We working in the next estate. Is crop-over time this week,
and we was running on the high road when the rain bar us.

CHANTAL

You can call me Tarzan.

OLD MAN

[*To* MOUMOU] And you, sir, what they call you? When
strangers in trouble so with rain, even by accident, is best
to make friends.

CHANTAL

Nothing is by accident I tell you, old man. That one, he cannot talk. *Un moumou,* you understand?

OLD MAN

Ay, *oui.* Sometimes is for the best. Is your brother, monsieur . . .

CHANTAL

Vidal. Yes, my brother. I cutting wood up there, you see? Past Regis boundary on the Crown lands, is hard work. And making coals too, to sell. Not in the rainy season. Up there is only myself and God sometimes.

OLD MAN

And your brother? He working?

CHANTAL

Yes. He is a spoon stealer. Ay you! The nephew! Give me a cigarette, if I have to answer this detective—what you are, old man, a bush magistrate? [NEPHEW *gives cigarettes*] *Alors!* Labourers, eh? *Alors, mes amis,* I mean you flush, today Saturday, half-day, crop-over on all estate. Maybe you and your uncle would buy a few spoons? Buy something for uncle, man. Look at it, look at it.

[*Draws out cutlass, places it on the ground*]

Nice silver spoon. Maybe a knife? To put in his back when he sleeping? Don't mind the *moumou,* is only buy he want to see you buy.

184

NEPHEW

We don't have that kind of money for true, Monsieur
Vidal.

OLD MAN

And even we buy, what we can eat with silver spoon?

CHANTAL

What you can eat? Rice, soup? How I know? Oh, you want
to know where I get the spoons, eh? Me. A poor woodcutter! I will tell you. My dead grandmother give them to me.
You have a dead grandmother, you know what they like.
They only want the best for you. Oh, look at them, the
poor and honest people, their purses tight as a crab's arse.
Buy it for your grandson, old man, and stick a silver spoon
in his mouth. Look it over all you want until the rain over.
And I have a silver cup too, perhaps you will want to give
the priest, holy man. [*Shouting to* MOUMOU] Sit down,
quiet mongoose!

OLD MAN

Monsieur Vidal, if my nephew and me can talk about this.
What to buy and so . . .

CHANTAL

Yes. Yes. The old full of wisdom. Talk your bargain, old
man. [OLD MAN *and* NEPHEW *draw aside*]

NEPHEW

What stupidness you talking?

185

OLD MAN

You see what the spoon mark?

NEPHEW

They could mark God self we not buying no spoon!

OLD MAN

You know who he is?

NEPHEW

Which one? The Moumou?

OLD MAN

With the big cloak. The woodcutter. That is Chantal the madman, the tiger out of prison! Chantal you hear about since you was a child!

[*Cymbals. Shouts off.* MAN *and* WIFE *running into the shed*]

HUSBAND

Jesus Marie La Vièrge en ciel avec per saecula seculorum, woy! Look at the rain! Charlemagne, Sonson! You all lucky you get here first. I am deadly soaked. *Bon Dieu,* these grains of rain bigger than mine. Messieurs, messieurs, messieurs! If you know what happen, old man. Excuse me, sirs. By Orangerie, you hear, me and Madeleine decide to take shelter under the old saman tree and wait for the P.W.D. truck. Well, by the time we reach there, I only hear *badow!* Force of lightning. Monsieur Charlemagne. Well, *hein,* if I was Moses I would say "Yes, God, that's right," but I ain't stop to see who win who lose. Madeleine and me take off whish, and behind us we only hear the saman tree falling abbragadangabasha. Like the fall of Babylon. Is a miracle I still alive! Well, well, when God snap His fingers sparks can fly eh? Never so frighten in my life before. Eh-eh, I didn't even see the strangers, pardon my manners, messieur, my name is Theophile Alexis alias Popo working by Boissiere estate, you hear how God spare my life?

CHANTAL

God have his days off too, m'sieur.

[*The* WIFE *removes her dress to dry*]

WIFE

Listen to the hypocrite, this good-for-nothing! As soon as is earthquake, hurricane or thunder, the first one to drop on his knees and cry God. [*To the* MOUMOU] Mind let me hang my dress, sir.

HUSBAND

I am the hypocrite? That lightning would make devil sweat cold. Of course I frighten, man cannot control thunder. And if you see the river, stranger, you know why my wife don't have nothing but a devil in she. It swelling more than a nine-month wife, carrying everything down the sea, branches in the road. Just as if the earth open and vomiting the dead like a grave. [*To* WIFE] Look at her, she don't have no shame, taking off her dress in front of strangers like a street woman.

[CHANTAL *takes out a piece of saltfish and chews it*]

WIFE

Those who have dirty minds will notice! I must leave on

this soaked dress to get a fever, eh? That's what you want, eh? That your wife could catch fever and die?

HUSBAND

Why don't you drink the bottle of *malcochon* the overseer give you to keep hot? The overseer give my wife a bottle of white rum for a bonus, and she treating it like is a baby she make. See how she wrap it up? You know Auguste the *shabin?* The red nigger that think he is a white man? Well, that bottle there, is he who give my wife. All of us working crop-over and we don't get no bonus. You get? You? Eh, *bien,* my wife, she get. If you ask her maybe she will give you to keep out the cold. Or what happen, nigger not suppose to drink it?

WIFE

Look at him! Look at him! The coward, the hypocrite. Just like a dog. In front of men he give jokes, he can shame his wife in front of strangers. Look at the brave dog that putting his tail between his legs for a flash of lightning. Making jokes now and wagging his tail for men to pat him on the back and say Popo the comic; why you don't tell them how you try and kill me in the rain on the high road, instead of making jokes about God? Is the bottle you want? Here! Drink it and show off!

HUSBAND

Who you calling dog, eh? Why you don't leave your coarseness for the house? When I try to kill you? You lie! you . . .

[*She wrings her dress out furiously*]

188

WIFE

Yes, yes, I lie! I lie then, dog. Look the rum, you don't want it? I never see a bigger fool in my life. He jealous of everything I do. If I laugh is to make my breasts shake, if I take off my dress not to catch fever, if I only . . . [*Turns away*]

HUSBAND

Cry now. As usual. Hypocrite. That one! Ah, if a man could only know . . .

OLD MAN

Popo, that is not the way to treat your wife in front of strangers.

HUSBAND

M'sieur, pardon, yes. But maybe you married too and have this kind of madness taking you. Is not any dog I am, but that half-coolie bitch there, because all the village praise her long hair and smooth skin, that is all she have in mind.

WIFE

Mentir! Mentir! Lies! Lies! Monsieur listen . . . !

[*The* MOUMOU *smiles*]

HUSBAND

Is not a joke when you suffering it, sir. For I don't laugh at people suffering . . .

NEPHEW

Uncle, let us go.

HUSBAND

I know I spoil this company. But when I ask her questions,
like any husband have a right to, she only shaking her hair
and laughing in my face and saying "Kill me, yes, kill me."
What kind of woman is that? What you can do with that
kind of woman?

CHANTAL

I not no judge, don't ask me. They say that waterfall there,
if you bathe in it full of sins, can make the truth come out.
If you sure is the truth you want I would chuck her in it,
but only if you can stand the truth! Maybe you should give
her a present, a few spoons? At least you can offer me and
my cousin here a drink from the rain?

HUSBAND

Is my wife own, sir.

CHANTAL

You see I come from spending six weeks there in the rain
forest on top the mountain cutting canoe wood with my son
here, and is long time I don't drink white rum with the human beast that is my brother, and with this dead dry saltfish and the cold rain getting colder, I would well like . . .

WIFE

Take it, you hear, sir.

[CHANTAL *takes the bottle and swallows*]

HUSBAND

Is true, man and woman could act like beasts sometimes.

190

Malcochon, or The Six in the Rain

Bourreaux, bourreaux, bêtes sauvages! God put beast and
spirit in all of us, and only God know why . . .

WIFE

God! God! Stop calling God! God didn't make you the dog
you are!

HUSBAND

And he didn't make you the whore you are!

CHANTAL

[*Singing*]

So help me God I going swell she belly
When the cassava grow!

[*Thunder and rain increasing*]

OLD MAN

Popo, take the advice of an old man who know suffering,
Who pass through storm and hatred, and all you all know
    it.
I see signs this morning from the time the sun get up,
And take off his blanket and walk up the mountain.
That this day would be trouble, like one of these days
When God will lose his patience and strike earth with light-
    ning,
Thunder and murder, and the bull-frog croak it . . .
A man must learn to love and forgive all that he love.
You know how my brother, how they hang him for that,
Is a madness that have no resolution except violence,
We not tigers and serpents and dogs, we are men.

[CHANTAL *gives the* MOUMOU *the bottle*]

We don't murder and curse, we leave the old savagery,
When you ask for justice make sure is not revenge,
And when you ask for truth make sure you don't mean jus-
    tice.
Is not the truth I am talking here, Monsieur Chantal?

NEPHEW

Papa!

    [*Thunder. All turn to* CHANTAL]

OLD MAN

I not 'fraid him.

CONTEUR

    [*Softly. Drums and flute, fast*]

Oy! The river bed come down,
The river bed come down,
The river bed come down,
And the dead turning over.

MUSICIANS

Waie! O waie O! The river bed come down,
And the dead turning over.

CONTEUR

The dead rolling over, the dead rolling over,
The rain coming down and it swelling the river!

Malcochon, or The Six in the Rain

MUSICIANS

Waie! O waie O! The rain swell the river,
And the dead rolling over!

CONTEUR

Waie!

[*Drum roll. Thunder. Pause*]

HUSBAND

Chantal?

OLD MAN

Chantal the madman. Tiger of the forest.

HUSBAND

[*Loud laughter, pointing*] This old man there with the
broken teeth and the crack voice, with one crooked eye and
marks on his face, this is Chantal the wood demon, that we
was frighten of as children? You remember, Sonson, when
we was boys together and playing till dark by the river or
in the bamboo, how we used to frighten one another with
this talk of Chantal? Chantal will hold you! Chantal passing through our village, so hide under the bed? Eat your
food or I will make Chantal hold you? And today this old
tiger with the *mange* begging me for a drink of *malcochon*
in the rain? That is what we was frighten of, Sonson? Look
at the devil, face to face! Tarzan of the apes, the enemy of
God. [*Picks up spoon and beats on his palm*] They had a
song they used to sing about him, yes, how it go again!
Tigre, Tigre, choux brulé! Tigre, tigre, choux. I go dead!

And now is as if you find out that life have nothing to be frighten of. As if the devil is a joke. Chantal? Chantal! Well I going dead! Believe me, I going dead. Madeleine, you don't hear . . .

WIFE

[*Pointing*] Aiieeeeee! Look! Look there! Bon Dieu! [*Covers her face with her hands*]

CONTEUR

[*Faster*]

The river bed coming down,
The river bed coming down,
The river bed coming down,
And a dead turning over!

[*The* MOUMOU *tries to run,* CHANTAL *grabs him, throwing him down*]

CHANTAL

Stay there, mongoose, you can't run now.

NEPHEW

What is it? What is it?

[*The* MOUMOU *starts whimpering*]

HUSBAND

Where the brown water coming down
As if the earth crack open and give birth to a dead.

WIFE

They have a dead man there, his body full of cuts
Like a axe will make, if a man was a tree,

Malcochon, or The Six in the Rain

A white man turning among loose water-lilies
Leaves on his face and turning in the water
Rolling in a muddy ditch going down to the sea.

NEPHEW

The force of the waterfall must be bring down the body.
But who is it? Who is it?

OLD MAN

Is Regis the planter.

WIFE

Look how it catch up among the black roots. A dead man, a
dead man, white cuts washed in rain!

OLD MAN

Oh God, I know from the way the thunder spoke,
And the writing of lightning, that disaster was in the sky,
That Bocage have a curse, and we all marked with it.

NEPHEW

The spoons! The spoons, Uncle!

HUSBAND

Which spoons you mean?

NEPHEW

The spoons marked R. Look! The spoons all marked R.

WIFE

Let us go, let us go. This place dark with rain.
We have nothing to do with it. Let's go home I tell you!

CHANTAL

Before anybody go home, we will hear confession.
You! The joker! Put down your cutlass there!
You too, mister, Nephew. And, woman, keep quiet.
Chantal will take confession. One and all, kneel down!

HUSBAND

Mister, they will hold you no matter what you do us.

NEPHEW

We are poor labourers together, we are the same people.

OLD MAN

Leave him alone, Nephew, and do what he tell you.
You say there is no evil any more, Monsieur Popo.
Well, look at the face of a beast that is drunk.
Look there and tremble, that face is the truth!

CHANTAL

You say enough, old man. From the time I here
I hear all four of you talking about the truth.
Well, I will give you the truth and see what you can do with
    it.
Chantal will take confession, now. One and all kneel down!
This rain will last long, and we have plenty time.

    [*They kneel*]

Saturday is a good day to die, is payday.
God resting on Sunday, and on Sunday in heaven.

    [*Drinks from the bottle*]

196

The priest, who know God personally, say is very quiet.

[*Kicks the* HUSBAND]

Ay! you! You seem to have a good memory of your child-
hood.
You know your catechism? You know the nine command-
ments?
Nine! Not ten. For as I am the judge here,
I leaving out the one that say thou shalt not steal.
Speak, husband. Or your head whistling from your neck
Like a coconut I steal when my belly making thunder.

HUSBAND

Let us go, Chantal. God say thou shalt not kill.

CHANTAL

You know a lot about what God say. God not a fool.
God know what man give for mankind is a beast,
The beast killed God son—the lamb! not so?
So what God means to say was "Thou should not kill,"
Knowing man will do it anyway, and the magistrate,
The priest and so on, they did not understand that.
But say your prayers, dog, while I confess your wife.

[*He strokes her shoulder*]

You! with the nice hair, you shaking in your husband face,
And always laughing "Kill me, kill me." You don't like
Chantal?
The old stinking tiger with broken teeth. I will tell you!
Let us go in the bamboo and he will show you the truth!
No? You prefer to die, eh, mistress? Well, say your confes-
sion.

197

This bottle of *malcochon* that the overseer give you . . .
You know the commandment "Thou shalt not make adultery"?

OLD MAN

Chantal, tiger. Have mercy on that one.

NEPHEW

Leave him alone! Leave him alone.
What you frighten of? The past, you and my mother?

WIFE

Is not true! Is not true!

[*Sobs. The* MOUMOU *moves to her*]

Moumou—ah. Is not true!

NEPHEW

They lie! They lie! On their death bed they will lie.
They have mothers who take their secret to the grave.
On their birth bed they lie. My father was right.

CHANTAL

You hear justice talking, woman? Well, now I pull your
    hair
And I show your bare neck. Go and sit down, mongoose.
I'll send a nice head for you to play with in your lap,
I lift up the cutlass and I . . .

WIFE

Is true! O God is true! Pardon, God is true! Don't kill me!
Is true, don't kill . . . Popo, Popo! [*She sobs*]

HUSBAND

I don't want to hear it! Kill me! I don't want to hear it!

NEPHEW

You see! True! True! Lies! Lies! all of them!

CHANTAL

Husband, I have a cutlass hanging over her neck. Pass
judgement, joker. Is the truth that you wanted.

HUSBAND

I am not God, Monsieur Chantal. And not a beast neither.

WIFE

Kill me, Chantal! Kill me! He cannot forgive.
I could never look in his face in my whole life again.
I cannot stand the shame of his forgiveness
Because even his forgiveness is part of his pride.
What am I to him? What he think of me now?
Don't ask him for mercy, because he will give it,
And boast about it always. Don't turn him into God!

HUSBAND

Madeleine, you cannot as a woman know a man;
I am a fool with ordinary sins.
Jealousy is one, and love is mixed with jealousy.
Jealousy is a disappointment, Madeleine,
That what we love is not perfect.
I love my wife, sir, and will be jealous of her
Till the day she is dead, and if God take her
And leave me on this earth, I will jealous of God.

What I saying is the truth. Don't cry, Madeleine.
You can cut my neck off, but that is the truth.

NEPHEW

Yes, yes, and tomorrow she will do it again.

OLD MAN

If you must kill somebody, kill me, old tiger!
Kill me. I am tired. And today I know the truth,
That this animal here who could be my own son
Could be a serpent from the hatred he have for me.
Kill me. Let the others go. I tired of this life,
And the rain crying for the sins of this world.

[*The* MOUMOU *gets up and is behind* CHANTAL]

CHANTAL

I drunk, friends. Drunk and hungry. I don't know what to
    do.
I always on the other side of the law. But life funny,
Today I must play judge. I will let you all go.
But if I let you all go, who will speak for Chantal?
All my life I just do what I want and leave the rest,
The responsibility, you follow, to the men who run the
    world,
The priest and magistrate, the rich man, the . . .

WIFE

Chantal! Look out! [*The* MOUMOU *plunges a cutlass into*
CHANTAL's *back*] Aiee!

[*They rise and draw back. The* MOUMOU *grins and shows
them the cutlass. He is trying to show that he has saved*

them. He goes to the woman, wipes the blood from his hands, and strokes her hair and dress]

HUSBAND

Don't scream, don't do anything, Madeleine. Take the cutlass from him, yes, and put it down. He think Chantal was going to kill us. Be brave. You see, he is smiling. Is think he think he save us.

[OLD MAN *bending over* CHANTAL]

OLD MAN

Chantal. Chantal . . .

NEPHEW

Let's go. Let's get out! The thunder passing.

OLD MAN

Go, beast, go. *Allez, bourreau!* Let men stay here. Your house is not my house.

NEPHEW

You fool. This man was trying to kill us just now.

HUSBAND

Make him sit down on the ground with you there, Madeleine. Poor beast. Poor animal. Yes, hold his hand and smile and talk to him. Like a child. As if he was a child.

[*The* MOUMOU *sits, puts his head in* MADELEINE's *lap*]

OLD MAN

He was trying to kill us, yes, and do your work for you.

How is it, old tiger? How are you, old tiger? It hurting you, my son?

CHANTAL

Tigre, tigre choux brulé. Tiger, tiger . . . That is you, old father? Who do it, the mongoose? You see how a man can have a good meaning and do the wrong thing?

OLD MAN

He think you was going to kill us.

CHANTAL

Maybe I was, maybe I was. I don't know, with all that rum in my head. Where is the mongoose?

OLD MAN

[*Holding him up*] Let me hold up your head. You see him over there, the woman have him quiet like a . . . a small dog.

CHANTAL

With a good heart. He have a good heart.

OLD MAN

He is a man, old tiger.

CHANTAL

Like a small dog he was, like a poor hungry dog with the fur falling off and you can see the ribs, that stealing and frighten—when I hear him in the bamboo thrashing around to hide, with the spoons under his arms and trying to hide. The other one had a gun, and he was turning round and round—mongoose looking for a hole in the world to hide . . . He thought I was going to kill you all, eh?

[*Sounds of a truck far off*]

HUSBAND

Madeleine, Charlemagne, Sonson, listen! You hear it, under the white noise of the water?

[*They wait. Silence*]

[*Noise of truck engine*]

HUSBAND

Is the engine of the Public Works truck passing on the high road. We have to go there and stop it. Come, Madeleine, take your dress, Charlemagne, Sonson.

CHANTAL

What they will do the mongoose? He cannot talk, make explanation, argue right and wrong with the magistrate . . .

NEPHEW

Is he who killed the white man?

CHANTAL

Ah yes, the one who always want the truth, the one who love justice before everything. Who will kill him? Who is the murderer, who the dead, eh, tell me . . . What use the truth is?

HUSBAND

The truck, the truck, *vieux cor'*.

Go with them. The rain is over.

No, no. Because you are my son. You are my brother. You are not the beast and the madman. No.

Leave him, old man. We will miss the truck!

Go, go! Leave me, I say! Go and meet it. You want me to bring you to the priest, old man?

[*They go out*]

Priest? What priest? What the priest can do now? What the priest know that Chantal don't know already? I spend my life with so much to send the priest crazy. I see and do things already in this world, in prison, in asylum, in the streets with this same old clothes, that the priest could fall asleep hearing the long list of my sins. What sins? I had a mad life but I don't sorry for nothing. I fix that up with God already in La Toc asylum and Victoria Hospital and Royal jail. I don't want to shock the priest and make him believe man can be so wicked. The priest might lose his faith listening to the madness of an old thief. Only God, who have a strong stomach and who is a very old man, an old rascal like me who frightening the world, could understand that, so don't mind about the priest. Only lift my head a little higher, old man, take off this old cap so the wind can blow the hairs on this bald head and I can look pass Bocage water to the cold mountain.

[*The truck blows. Shouts far off*]

Look how it wet and green with the wind blowing. Three years I working there, and sometime in the morning when the sun coming up, I did only feel to roar like a mad tiger. "Praise be God in His excellence!" And look at the sun making diamond on the wet leaves. That's all the money I ever had in this life. A man should not leave that forest, eh?

OLD MAN

Man have to live with man, Chantal.

[*Truck horn. Music*]

CONTEUR

[*To slow flute and drum*]

Like the staining of clear springs the mind of man,
In blood he must end as in blood he began
Like mist that rises from a muddy stream
Between beasthood and Godhead groping in a dream.

OLD MAN

Chantal?

CHANTAL

In the forest there in the rainy mountain where no man was, I was a happy old man, just me and old God. But man have a time to come down. Lift me higher, old man, and I will show you something. You see that place there, a little clearing there in the side of the mountain, that Chantal cut out of the forest? There where a chicken hawk shaking rain from its wing and flying over the valley to the other side of the clouds . . .

OLD MAN

I see the place, old tiger, but the hawk gone now.

CHANTAL

Is there I come from this morning, it look far, eh? It look so far now, and the mist closing it. [*Dies*]

OLD MAN

No so far, Chantal. Not far at all, my son.

> [*Truck blowing impatiently.* OLD MAN *rests* CHANTAL *down*]

CONTEUR

> [*Faster flute and drum*]

The rage of the beast is taken for granted,
Man's beauty is sharing his brother's pain;
God sends the wound where a wound is wanted,
This is the story of six in the rain.

> [*Thunder far off. Flute fading*]

CURTAIN

Dream on Monkey Mountain

FOR ERROL JONES AND
THE TRINIDAD THEATRE WORKSHOP

*If the moon is earth's friend,
how can we leave the earth?*
Noh Play

A Note on Production

The play is a dream, one that exists as much in the given minds of its principal characters as in that of its writer, and as such, it is illogical, derivative, contradictory. Its source is metaphor and it is best treated as a physical poem with all the subconscious and deliberate borrowings of poetry. Its style should be spare, essential as the details of a dream. The producer can amplify it with spectacle as he chooses, or, as in the original production, switch roles and limit his cast to a dozen or so. He will need dancers, actors, and singers, the same precision and vitality that one has read of in the Kabuki. He may add songs more recognisable to his audience once he can keep the raw folk content in them. Scene 11, the healing scene, owes an obvious debt to "Spirit," choreographed for the Little Carib Company by Beryl MacBurnie.

D. W.

CHARACTERS

TIGRE, a felon

SOURIS, a felon

CORPORAL LESTRADE, a mulatto

MAKAK, a charbonnier or charcoal-burner

APPARITION, the moon, the muse, the white Goddess, a dancer

MOUSTIQUE, a cripple, friend to Makak

BASIL, a cabinet-maker, figure of death

MARKET INSPECTOR PAMPHILION, a government servant

A DANCER, also NARRATOR

LITTER BEARERS

SISTERS OF THE REVELATION

MARKET WOMEN, WIVES OF MAKAK

A singer, a male chorus, two drummers

(The play was first produced at the Central Library Theatre, To-
ronto, on August 12, 1967, with the following cast: Joel St. Helene
as the DANCER; Albert LeVeau as BASIL; Sydney Best as TIGRE; Hamil-
ton Parris as SOURIS; Ralph Campbell as CORPORAL LESTRADE; Errol
Jones as MAKAK; Stanley Marshall as MOUSTIQUE; Eunice Alleyne,
Lynette LeVeau, Elena James, and Marcia Slaney as SISTERS OF THE
REVELATION; Elena James as the APPARITION; Claude Reid, Terence
Joseph, Sydney Best, and Hamilton Parris as LITTER BEARERS; Joel St.
Helene as the SICK MAN; Claude Reid as INSPECTOR PAMPHILION;
Eunice Alleyne, Lynette LeVeau, Elena James, and Marcia Slaney as
PEASANT WOMEN; Hamilton Parris, Sydney Best, Terence Joseph, and
Joel St. Helene as WARRIORS. The lighting was by John Andrews and
the décor by Derek Walcott and Leroy Clarke.)

SETTING

A West Indian Island

Part One

Thus in certain psychoses the hallucinated person, tired of always being insulted by his demon, one fine day starts hearing the voice of an angel who pays him compliments; but the jeers don't stop for all that; only, from then on, they alternate with congratulations. This is a defence, but it is also the end of the story. The self is disassociated, and the patient heads for madness.

Sartre: Prologue to "The Wretched of the Earth," by Frantz Fanon

Prologue

A spotlight warms the white disc of an African drum until it glows like the round moon above it. Below the moon is the stark silhouette of a volcanic mountain. Reversed, the moon becomes the sun. A dancer enters and sits astride the drum. From the opposite side of the stage a top-hatted, frock-coated figure with white gloves, his face halved by white make-up like the figure of Baron Samedi, enters and crouches behind the dancer. As the lament begins, dancer and figure wave their arms slowly, sinuously, with a spidery motion. The figure rises during the lament and touches the disc of the moon. The drummer rises, dancing as if in slow motion, indicating, as their areas grow distinct, two prison cages on either side of the stage. In one cell, TIGRE and SOURIS, two half-naked felons are squabbling. The figure strides off slowly, the CONTEUR and CHORUS, off-stage, increase the volume of their lament.

CONTEUR

Mooma, mooma,
Your son in de jail a'ready,
Your son in de jail a'ready,
Take a towel and
                   band your belly.

CHORUS

Mooma, mooma,
Your son in de jail a'ready,
Your son in de jail a'ready,
Take a towel and
                    band your belly.

CONTEUR

I pass by the police station,
Nobody to sign de bail bond.

CHORUS

Mooma, don't cry,
Your son in de jail a'ready,
I pass by de police station,
Nobody to sign de bail bond.

CONTEUR

Forty days before the Carnival, Lord,
I dream I see me funeral.

CHORUS

Mooma, mooma,
Your son in de jail a'ready,
Take a towel and band your belly.

> [*The* CORPORAL, *in Sunday uniform, enters with* MAKAK,
> *an old Negro with a jute sack, and lets him into the next
> cell*]

TIGRE

Forty days before the Carnival,
Lord, I dream I see me funeral . . .

TIGRE AND SOURIS

Mooma, don't cry, your son in de jail a'ready . . .

TIGRE

Take a towel and band you' belly,
Mooma, don't cry, your son in de jail a'ready.

[MAKAK *sits on the cell cot, an old cloth around his shoulders*]

SOURIS

Shut up! Ay, Corporal. Who is dat?

TIGRE

[*Singing*]

Mooma, don't cry, your son in de jail a'ready.

CORPORAL

Dat, you mange-ridden habitual felon, is de King of Africa.

TIGRE

[*Singing*]

Your son in de jail a'ready,
Your son in de jail a'ready . . .

SOURIS

Tigre, shut your trap. It have Majesty there.

[*The* CORPORAL *elaborately removes a notebook and gold pencil*]

CORPORAL

Now before I bring a specific charge against you, I will require certain particulars . . .

TIGRE, SOURIS AND CORPORAL

You are required by law to supply me with certain data, for no man is guilty except so proven, and I must warn you that anything you say may be held against you . . .

CORPORAL

[*Turning*] Look!

SOURIS

Don't tell him a damn thing! You have legal rights. Your lawyer! Get your lawyer.

TIGRE

[*Singing*]

I pass by de police station,
Nobody to sign de bail bond,
Mooma, don't cry . . .

SOURIS

[*Shrilly*] What he up for, Corporal? What you lock him up for?

CORPORAL

Drunk and disorderly! A old man like that! He was drunk and he mash up Alcindor café.

215

SOURIS

And you going cage him here on a first offence? Old man,
get a lawyer and defend your name!

> [*The* CORPORAL *bends down and removes a half-empty*
> *bottle of rum from the bag, and a white mask with long*
> *black sisal hair*]

CORPORAL

I must itemize these objects! Can you identify them?

SOURIS

O God, O God, Tigre! The king got a bottle! [SOURIS *and*
TIGRE *grope through the bars, howling, groaning*] O God,
just one, Corporal. My throat on fire. One for the boys.
Here, just one swallow, Corp.

TIGRE

Have mercy on two thieves fallen by the wayside. You call
yourself a Catholic?

> [*Inchoate, animal howling, leaping and pacing*]

CORPORAL

Animals, beasts, savages, cannibals, niggers, stop turning
this place to a stinking zoo!

SOURIS

Zoo? Just because you capture some mountain gorilla?

> [*The* CORPORAL *with his baton cracks* SOURIS's *extended*
> *wrist*]

CORPORAL

In the beginning was the ape, and the ape had no name,

so God call him man. Now there were various tribes of the
ape, it had gorilla, baboon, orang-outan, chimpanzee, the
blue-arsed monkey and the marmoset, and God looked at
his handiwork, and saw that it was good. For some of the
apes had straighten their backbone, and start walking upright, but there was one tribe unfortunately that lingered
behind, and that was the nigger. Now if you apes will behave like gentlemen, who knows what could happen? The
bottle could go round, but first it behoves me, Corporal
Lestrade, to perform my duty according to the rules of Her
Majesty's Government, so don't interrupt. Please let me
examine the Lion of Judah. [*Goes towards* MAKAK] What
is your name?

TIGRE

[*Singing softly*]

Oh, when the roll
Is called up yonder,
When the roll
Is called up yonder,
When the roll
Is called up yonder,
When the roll is called up yonder,
I ain't going!

[CHORUS: *When the roll* . . .]

[*Spoken*] And nobody else here going, you all too black,
except possibly the Corporal. [*Pauses, points*] Look, is the
full moon.

217

CORPORAL

[*As moonlight fills the cell*] Your name in full, occupation, status, income, ambition, domicile or place of residence, age, and last but not least, your race?

SOURIS

The man break my hand. The damn man break my hand.

TIGRE

Well, you can't t'hief again.

MAKAK

Let me go home, my Corporal.

SOURIS

Ay, wait, Tigre, the king has spoken.

TIGRE

What the king say?

SOURIS

He want to go home.

CORPORAL

Where is your home? Africa?

MAKAK

Sur Morne Macaque . . .

CORPORAL

[*Infuriated*] English, English! For we are observing the

principles and precepts of Roman law, and Roman law is
English law. Let me repeat the query: Where is your home?

MAKAK

I live on Monkey Mountain, Corporal.

CORPORAL

What is your name?

MAKAK

I forget.

CORPORAL

What is your race?

MAKAK

I am tired.

CORPORAL

What is your denominational affiliation?

[*Silence*]

SOURIS

[*Whispering*] *Ça qui religion-ous?*

MAKAK

[*Smiling*] Cat'olique.

CORPORAL

I ask you, with all the patience of the law, what is or has
been your denominational affiliation?

MAKAK

Cat'olique.

CORPORAL

[*Revising notes*] You forget your name, your race is tired, your denominational affiliation is Catholique, therefore, as the law, the Roman law, had pity on our Blessed Saviour, by giving him, even *in extremis,* a draught of vinegar, what, in your own language, you would call *vinegre,* I shall give all and sunday here, including these two thieves, a handful of rum, before I press my charge.

> [TIGRE *and* SOURIS *applaud loudly. The* CORPORAL *takes a swallow from the bottle and passes it through the bars to* TIGRE *and* SOURIS; *then, holding it in his hand, paces around* MAKAK]

TIGRE

How a man like that can know so much law? Could know so much language? Is a born Q.C. Still every man entitle to his own defence.

SOURIS

The wig and gown, Corporal. Put on the wig and gown!

TIGRE

You have a sense of justice, put on the wig and gown.

CORPORAL

I can both accuse and defend this man.

SOURIS

The wig and gown, Lestrade. Let us hear English!

[*The* CORPORAL *strides off*]

SOURIS

[*Sings*]

Drill him, Constable, drill him,
Drill him, Constable, drill him,
Drill him, Constable, drill him.
He t'ief a bag of coals yesterday!

CHORUS

[*Repeats*]

Drill him, Constable, drill him . . .

SOURIS

Drill him, Constable, drill him,
He mash up old Alcindor café!

[*The* CORPORAL, *isolated in a spot, with counsel's wig and gown, returns with four towels, two yellow, two red*]

TIGRE

Order, order, order in de court.

[*A massive gong is sounded, and the* CORPORAL *gives the two prisoners the towels. They robe themselves like judges*]

CORPORAL

My noble judges. When this crime has been categorically examined by due process of law, and when the motive of the hereby accused by whereas and ad hoc shall be established without dychotomy, and long after we have perambulated through the labyrinthine bewilderment of the defendant's ignorance, let us hope, that justice, whom we all serve, will not only be done, but will appear, my lords, to have itself, been done . . . [*The* JUDGES *applaud*] Ignorance is no excuse. Ignorance of the law is no excuse. Ignorance of one's own ignorance is no excuse. This is the prisoner. I will ask the prisoner to lift up his face. *Levez la tête-ous!*

> [MAKAK *lifts up his head. The* CORPORAL *jerks it back savagely*]

CORPORAL

My lords, as you can see, this is a being without a mind, a will, a name, a tribe of its own. I shall ask the prisoner to turn out his hands. *Montrez-moi la main-ous!* [MAKAK *turns his palm outward*] I will spare you the sound of that voice, which have come from a cave of darkness, dripping with horror. These hands are the hands of Esau, the fingers are like roots, the arteries as hard as twine, and the palms are seamed with coal. But the animal, you observe, is tamed and obedient. Walk round the cage! *Marchez! Marchez!*

> [MAKAK *rises and walks round the bench, as the* CHORUS *begins to sing*]

CHORUS

I don't know what to say this monkey won't do,
I don't know what to say this monkey won't do.

> [*As the* CORPORAL, *like an animal tamer, cracks out his orders, the choir of* JUDGES *keeps time, clapping*]

CORPORAL

About turn!

[MAKAK *turns around wearily*]

CHORUS

Cause when I turn round, monkey turn around too,
I don't know what to say this monkey won't do.

CORPORAL

On your knees!

> [MAKAK *drops to his knees.* SOURIS *shrieks with delight,
> then collects his dignity*]

I kneel down, monkey kneel down too,
I don't know what to say this monkey won't do.
I praying, monkey praying too,
I don't know what the hell this monkey won't do.

CORPORAL

Stand up! Sit down! Up on the bench! Sit down! Hands
out! Hands in!

> [MAKAK *does all this. The* CHORUS *sings faster, and the*
> JUDGES *keep time*]

CHORUS

Everything I say this monkey does do,
I don't know what to say this monkey won't do.
I sit down, monkey sit down too,
I don't know what to say this monkey won't do.

> [MAKAK *sits wearily on the bench*]

CORPORAL

[*Holds up a palm*] The exercise, my lords, prove that the

prisoner is capable of reflexes, of obeying orders, therefore of understanding justice. Sound body. Now the charge!

[*Drum roll*]

[*To the sound of martial drums*] His rightful name is unknown, yet on Saturday evening, July 25th, to wit tonight, at exactly three hours ago, to wit at 5:30 p.m., having tried to dispose of four bags of charcoal in the market of Quatre Chemin, to wit this place, my lords, in which aforesaid market your alias, to wit Makak, is well known to all and sunday, the prisoner, in a state of incomprehensible intoxication, from money or moneys accrued by the sale of self-said bags, is reputed to have entered the licenced alcoholic premises of one Felicien Alcindor, whom the prisoner described as an agent of the devil, the same Felicien Alcindor being known to all and sunday as a God-fearing, honest Catholic. [*He rests the bottle down*] When some intervention was attempted by those present, the prisoner then began to become vile and violent; he engaged in a blasphemous, obscene debate with two other villagers, Hannibal Dolcis and Market Inspector Caiphas Joseph Pamphilion, describing in a foul, incomprehensible manner . . .

[*The* JUDGES *posture: Hear no evil. Hands to their ears*]

a dream which he claims to have experienced, a vile, ambitious, and obscene dream . . .

[*The* JUDGES *mime: See no evil. Hands to their faces in horror*]

elaborating on the aforesaid dream with vile words and with a variety of sexual obscenities both in language and posture! Further, the prisoner, in defiance of Her Majesty's

Government, urged the aforementioned villagers to join him in sedition and the defilement of the flag, and when all this was rightly received with civic laughter and pious horror . . .

[*The* JUDGES *mime: Speak no evil. Their hands to their mouths*]

the prisoner, in desperation and shame, began to wilfully damage the premises of the proprietor Felicien Alcindor, urging destruction on Church and State, claiming that he was the direct descendant of African kings, a healer of leprosy and the Saviour of his race.

[*Pause. Silence*]

You claimed that with the camera of your eye you had taken a photograph of God and all that you could see was blackness.

[*The* JUDGES *rise in horror*]

Blackness, my lords. What did the prisoner imply? That God was neither white nor black but nothing? That God was not white but black, that he had lost his faith? Or . . . or . . . what . . .

MAKAK

I am an old man. Send me home, Corporal. I suffer from madness. I does see things. Spirits does talk to me. All I have is my dreams and they don't trouble your soul.

TIGRE

I can imagine your dreams. Masturbating in moonlight.

Dreaming of women, cause you so damn ugly. You should walk on all fours.

MAKAK

Sirs, I does catch fits. I fall in a frenzy every full-moon night. I does be possessed. And after that, sir, I am not responsible. I responsible only to God who once speak to me in the form of a woman on Monkey Mountain. I am God's warrior.

[*The* JUDGES *laugh*]

CORPORAL

You are charged with certain things. Now let the prisoner make his deposition.

MAKAK

[*During this speech, the cage is raised out of sight*]

Sirs, I am sixty years old. I have live all my life
Like a wild beast in hiding. Without child, without wife.
People forget me like the mist on Monkey Mountain.
Is thirty years now I have look in no mirror,
Not a pool of cold water, when I must drink,
I stir my hands first, to break up my image.
I will tell you my dream. Sirs, make a white mist
In the mind; make that mist hang like cloth
From the dress of a woman, on prickles, on branches,
Make it rise from the earth, like the breath of the dead
On resurrection morning, and I walking through it
On my way to my charcoal pit on the mountain.
Make the web of the spider heavy with diamonds

226

And when my hand brush it, let the chain break.
I remember, in my mind, the cigale sawing,
Sawing, sawing wood before the woodcutter,
The drum of the bull-frog, the blackbird flute,
And this old man walking, ugly as sin,
In a confusion of vapour,
Till I feel I was God self, walking through cloud.
In the heaven on my mind. Then I hear this song.
Not the blackbird flute,
Not the bull-frog drum,
Not the whistling of parrots
As I brush through the branches, shaking the dew,
A man swimming through smoke,
And the bandage of fog unpeeling my eyes,
As I reach to this spot,
I see this woman singing
And my feet grow roots. I could move no more.
A million silver needles prickle my blood,
Like a rain of small fishes.
The snakes in my hair speak to one another,
The smoke mouth open, and I behold this woman,
The loveliest thing I see on this earth,
Like the moon walking along her own road.

[*During this, the apparition appears and withdraws*]

[*Flute music*]

MAKAK

You don't see her? Look, I see her! She standing right
there. [*He points at nothing*] Like the moon had climbed
down the steps of heaven, and was standing in front me.

CORPORAL

I can see nothing. [*To the* JUDGES] What do you see?

JUDGES

Nothing. Nothing.

MAKAK

Nothing? Look, there she is!

TIGRE

Nothing at all. The old man mad.

SOURIS

[*Mocking*] Yes, I see it. I can see it. Is the face of the moon moving over the floor. Come to me, darling. [*He rolls over the cell floor groaning*]

CORPORAL

My lords, is this rage for whiteness that does drive niggers mad.

MAKAK

[*On his knees*]

Lady in heaven, is your old black warrior,
The king of Ashanti, Dahomey, Guinea,
Is this old cracked face you kiss in his sleep
Appear to my enemies, tell me what to do?
Put on my rage, the rage of the lion?

[*He rises slowly and assumes a warrior's stance. Drums build to a frenzy*]

Help poor crazy Makak, help Makak
To scatter his enemies, to slaughter those
That standing around him.
So, thy hosts shall be scattered,
And the hyena shall feed on their bones!

[*He falls*]

Sirs, when I hear that voice,
Singing so sweetly,
I feel my spine straighten,
My hand grow strong.
My blood was boiling
Like a brown river in flood,
And in that frenzy,
I let out a cry,
I charged the spears about me,
Grasses and branches,
I began to dance,
With the splendour of a lion,
Faster and faster,
Faster and faster,
Then, my body sink,
My bones betray me
And I fall on the forest floor,
Dead, on sweating grass,
And there, maybe, sirs,
Two other woodmen find me,
And take me up the track.
Sirs, if you please . . .

[*The two prisoners carry him*]

CORPORAL

Continue, continue, the virtue of the law is its infinite patience. Continue . . .

[*The cells rise, the others withdraw.* MAKAK *lies alone in the hut*]

Scene One

MAKAK remains on the ground, the mask near him. We hear a cry far off, echoing. MOUSTIQUE, a little man with a limp, a jute bag over his shoulder, comes into the morning light around the hut, puffing with exhaustion.

MOUSTIQUE

Makak, Makak, wake up. Is me, Moustique. You didn't hear me calling you from the throat of the gully? I bring a next crocus bag from Alcindor café. Today is market day, and time and tide wait for no man. I tie Berthilia to a gommier tree by the ravine.

[MAKAK *has stirred*]

MAKAK

Berthilia? Which Berthilia?

MOUSTIQUE

Listen to him! Which Berthilia? The donkey you and I buy from Felicien! Every Saturday is the same damn trouble to wake you! You have the coals ready, eh? Spare me a little to light this fire. [*He helps* MAKAK *into the hut*] Ay, what? What happen? [*He stoops near him*] Eh! Negre? [*He rests the back of his hand on* MAKAK's *forehead*] No fever.

231

No sweat. [*He walks around the hut, distressed*] What we going to do? The last time this happen, I find you outside the hut, trembling with fever. What we going do? [*He throws down the bag*]

MAKAK

Go alone.

MOUSTIQUE

Go alone? Tcha, go alone.

MAKAK

I going mad, Moustique.

MOUSTIQUE

Going mad? Go mad tomorrow, today is market day. We have three bags at three-and-six a bag, making ten shillings and sixpence for the week and you going mad? You have coffee?

MAKAK

I don't want.

MOUSTIQUE

Well, I want, I cold like hell. [MOUSTIQUE *prepares coffee and sits down pensively by the small fire, watching the water boil. He takes out a pipe and sighs*]

MAKAK

Moustique?

MOUSTIQUE

Eh?

MAKAK

How many years I know you now?

MOUSTIQUE

[*Shrugs*] Three, four. Why? [*He is making the coffee*]

MAKAK

You find that long?

MOUSTIQUE

[*Turns, stares at him*] No. [*Pause*] Look, we going to the market?

MAKAK

Yes. We will go.

MOUSTIQUE

[*Crouched on his heels, poking the fire*] Well, I just getting you something hot to drink. [*Leans back, puffs on his pipe*] Four years. And I remember how you find me.

MAKAK

True?

MOUSTIQUE

True. Drunk. Soaking drunk, with this twist foot God give me. Sleeping anywhere, and one morning when you come to market, you find me in the gutter, and you pick me up like a wet fly in the dust, and we establish in this charcoal business. You cut, burn and so on, and I sell, until we make enough to buy the donkey. [*Stretches for the coffee*]

233

Here, pass the cup. [*Pours*] Yes. You was the only one to make me believe a breakfoot nigger could go somewhere in this life. Four years gone last August. Drink. [*He passes the cup*] Drink. But after that is zwip! down the mountain!

MAKAK

[*Staring into the cup*] Moustique . . .

MOUSTIQUE

[*Patiently*] Ehhh?

MAKAK

Listen. You take the same short-cut to come up here?

MOUSTIQUE

Oui.

MAKAK

The one with the wood-bridge and white falling-water?

MOUSTIQUE

The one with the wood-bridge and white falling-water.

MAKAK

The one that so narrow, two men cannot pass?

MOUSTIQUE

The one that so narrow, two men . . . Drink.

[*Sound of a flute, bird noises*]

MAKAK

[*Rising*] This morning, early, the moon still up, I went to

234

pack the coals in the pit down the mountain. I will tell you. Make a white mist in the mind; make that mist hang like cloth from the dress of a woman, on prickles, on branches; make it rise from the earth, like the breath of the dead on resurrection morning, and I walking through it on my way to my charcoal pit on the mountain. Make the web of the spider be heavy with diamonds and when my hand brush it, let the chain break. I remember, in my mind, the cigale sawing, sawing, sawing wood before the woodcutter, the drum of the bull-frog, the blackbird flute, and this old man walking, ugly as sin, in a confusion of vapour, till I feel I was God self, walking through cloud, in the heaven of my mind. Then I hear this song. Not the bull-frog drum, not the whistling of parrots. As I brush through the branches, shaking the dew, a man swimming through smoke, and the bandage of fog unpeeling my eyes, as I reach to this spot, I see this woman singing, and my feet grow roots! I could move no more. A million silver needles prickle my blood, like a rain of small fishes. The snakes in my hair speak to one another, the smoke mouth open, and I behold this woman, the loveliest thing I see on this earth, floating towards me, just like the moon, like the moon walking along her own road. Then as I start to move, she call out my name, my real name. A name I do not use. Come here, she say. Come, don't be afraid. So I go up to her, one step by one step. She make me sit down and start to talk to me.

MOUSTIQUE
Makak.

235

MAKAK

[*Angrily*] Listen to me, I not mad. Listen!

MOUSTIQUE

I have all day. [*Exasperated*]

MAKAK

Well, well . . . the things she tell me, you would not believe. She did know my name, my age, where I born, and that it was charcoal I burn and selling for a living. She know how I live alone, with no wife and no friend . . .

MOUSTIQUE

No friend . . .

MAKAK

That Makak is not my name. And I tell her my life, and she say that if I want her, she will come and live with me, and I take her in my arms, and I bring her here.

MOUSTIQUE

[*Looking around*] Here? A white woman? Or a *diablesse?*

MAKAK

We spend all night here. Look, I make something for she to eat. We sit down by this same fire. And, Moustique, she say something I will never forget. She say I should not live so any more, here in the forest, frighten of people because I think I ugly. She say that I come from the family of lions and kings.

[*Drum roll*]

MOUSTIQUE

Well, you lucky. [*Rises wearily*] Me and Berthilia have
three bags of coal to try and sell in the market this morning. We still have eighteen shillings for Alcindor for the
shovel, and Johannes promise us a bag of provisions in exchange for half a sack. You had a bad dream, or you sleep
outside and the dew seize you.

MAKAK

Is not a dream.

MOUSTIQUE

[*Exasperated*] Is not a dream? Then where she? Where she
gone? [*Searches mockingly*] Upstairs? *Gadez!* You had a
dream, and she is here [*Touches his own head*], so, bring
her to market. Sun hot, and people making money.

MAKAK

I tell you is no dream.

MOUSTIQUE

You remember one morning I come up and from the time
I break the bush, I see you by the side of the hut, trembling
and talking, your eyes like you crazy, and was I had
to gather bush, light a fire and make you sweat out that
madness? Which white lady? You is nothing. You black,
ugly, poor, so you worse than nothing. You like me. Small,
ugly, with a foot like a "S." Man together two of us is mi-
nus one. Now where you going?

MAKAK

I going to get the coals [MAKAK *goes out,* MOUSTIQUE *cleans up, talking to himself*]

MOUSTIQUE

The misery black people have to see in this life. [*Rummaging around, blowing out the fire, putting away the cups*] Him and his damned fits. A man not only suppose to catch his arse in the daytime but he have to ride nightmares too. Now what the hell I looking for? [*He puts his hand under the bench, then withdraws it slowly in horror*] Aiiiiiiiiiiie. [*He turns his head and shakes his hand in frenzy as* MAKAK *comes running into the hut*].

MAKAK

Moustique!

MOUSTIQUE

[*Shaken*] A spider. A spider was on the sack. A big white one with eggs. A mother with white eggs. I hate those things.

MAKAK

Where it?

MOUSTIQUE

Look it. Kill it, kill it. [*Grabs his hat and pounds it*] Salop! Salop! When it pass over my hand, my blood turn into a million needles. [*He sits back panting*] Well. What you looking at? [*Pause*] Is a bad sign?

238

MAKAK

Yes, is a bad sign.

MOUSTIQUE

Well?

MAKAK

You know what it mean.

MOUSTIQUE

Yes. [*Holds out his hand, which is trembling*] To hell with
that! I don't believe that. I not no savage. Every man have
to die. It have a million ways to die. But no spider with
white eggs will bring it. [*Silence*] You believe that, of
course. You . . . you . . . you living like a beast, and you
believe everything! [*Points at the spider*] That! [*Stamps on
it*]

MAKAK

She say I will see signs.

MOUSTIQUE

Yes, every damned full moon.

MAKAK

I must do what she say, which is . . .

MOUSTIQUE

Which is to sell coals! Now, where the next sack? [*He
searches under the bench and withdraws a white mask with
long coarse hair*] This is she? eh? This cheap stupidness

black children putting on? [*He puts it on, wiggles and dances*] Chatafunga, deux sous pour weh, Chatafunga, deux sous pour weh.

[MAKAK *steps back*]

MAKAK

Where you get that?

MOUSTIQUE

You ain't see?

MAKAK

[*Slowly*] I never see it before.

MOUSTIQUE

She leave her face behind. She leave the wrong thing. Ah, Mon Dieu. [*He sits by the fire, puffing his pipe angrily, pokes the fire*] And the damned fire out.

MAKAK

I never see this before. [*Pause*] Saddle my horse!

MOUSTIQUE

Eh?

MAKAK

Saddle my horse, if you love me, Moustique, and cut a sharp bamboo for me, and put me on that horse, for Makak will ride to the edge of the world, Makak will walk like he used to in Africa, when his name was lion!

240

MOUSTIQUE

Saddle your horse? Berthilia the jackass? When you will put sense in that crack coal-pot you call your head? Which woman ever look at you, once, much less a white one? Saddle your horse? I could put this beat-up tin pot on your head, cut a bamboo for a spear, make a cup of my two hands and put you on that half-starve jackass you call a horse and send you out for the whole world to laugh. But where we going? Where two black, not-a-red-cent niggers going? To war?

MAKAK

Non. To Africa!

MOUSTIQUE

Oh-o! Africa? Why you didn't tell me? We walking? [*He stands in the doorway.* MAKAK *hurls him away*]

MAKAK

Out of my way, insect!

MOUSTIQUE

[*On the floor*] You mad. To God, you mad, O God, the day come, when I see you mad. [MAKAK *crouches over him.* MOUSTIQUE *is weeping*]

MAKAK

I hurt you, little one? Listen, listen, Moustique. I am not mad. To God, I am not mad. You say once when I pick you up like a wet fly from the dust that you would do anything for me. I beg you now, come. Don't cry! You say we will be friends until we dead. Come, don't mind the spider. If we dead, little one, is not better to die, fighting like men, than to hide in this forest? Come, then, lean on Makak. Bring nothing, we will live. [MAKAK, *who has helped* MOUSTIQUE *to his feet, takes up the bamboo spear, and goes out of the hut*]

MOUSTIQUE

Yes, yes, master. [MOUSTIQUE *puts out the fire, picks up the sacks, stool, then the mask, and looking at the squashed spider, shudders*] What is to come, will come. Come on, down the mountain.

[*The hut rises out of sight,* MAKAK *striding with his spear,* MOUSTIQUE *riding ahead*]

MOUSTIQUE

Is the stupidest thing I ever see
Two jackasses and one donkey,
Makak turn lion, so let him pass,
Donkey gone mad on pangola grass,
Haw haw haw haw haw haw hee,
A man not a man without misery,
Down the mountain!

[*Sound of the jackass braying*]

MAKAK and MOUSTIQUE set out, MAKAK striding ahead; MOUSTIQUE, to the rhythm of flute and drum, miming the donkey. The dancer doing the *burroquite,* or donkey dance, circles the stage and turns the disc of the sun to moonlight. The lights dim briefly, just long enough to establish a change of mood.

Scene Two

There is a sound of wailing. White-robed women, members of a sister-hood, bearing torches, swirl onto the stage, which is now a country road. Behind them, carrying a shrouded SICK MAN in a bamboo hammock, are four bearers and a tall frock-coated man in black silk hat, BASIL, his face halved by white make-up. The SISTERS, shaking their heads, dancing solemnly and singing, form a circle described by their leader. The bearers turn and rest the SICK MAN down. Around him, the SISTERS kneel and pray, swaying, trying to exorcise his sickness. A small fire is lit by the bearers. The silk-hatted man stands back quietly, watching, while the SISTERS clap and sing.

SISTERS
Before this time another year
I may be gone, Lord,
In some lonesome graveyard
Oh Lord, how long?

MOUSTIQUE
[*Enters*] Good night. God bless you, brother.

FIRST PEASANT
Shh. God bless you, stranger. Pray with us.

243

MOUSTIQUE

[*Crosses himself, prays swiftly, then in the same whisper*]
. . . And give us this day our daily bread . . . and is that
self I want to talk to you about, friend. Whether you could
spare a little bread . . . and lead us not into temptation
. . . because we are not thieves, stranger . . . but deliver
us from evil . . . and we two trespassers but forgive us
brother . . . for thine is the kingdom and the power and
the glory . . . for our stomach sake, stranger.

FIRST PEASANT

[*Keeping the whisper*] Where you come from, stranger
. . . now and at the hour of our death, amen.

MOUSTIQUE

[*Whispering*] From Monkey Mountain, in Forestiere quarter . . . and forgive us our trespasses . . . amen, is me
and my friend and old man . . . in the name of the father
. . . and we was sleeping in a hut by the road there, when
we see you all coming, with all those lights, I thought it was
the devil.

FIRST PEASANT

. . . Now and at the hour of our death, amen. . . . It
ain't have much to eat, stranger. We taking the sick man
down to the hospital, and it have just enough for all of us
here . . . forever and ever, amen.

MOUSTIQUE

[*In a fiercer whisper*] . . . Our daily bread, and forgive us
our trespasses . . . Anything, brother. Three days now we

travelling on these roads. What is wrong with him, stranger?

FIRST PEASANT

A snake. He was working in the bush, and a snake . . . but deliver us from evil . . . and no medicine can cure him.

MOUSTIQUE

So what they doing him now?

FIRST PEASANT

. . . And at the hour of our death, amen . . . they putting coals under his body to make him sweat. To break the heat in his body so he can sweat . . . forever and ever, amen . . . so they making a small fire to break the sweat with coals.

MOUSTIQUE

Coals?

FIRST PEASANT

Charcoal. You ent know charcoal?

MOUSTIQUE

Charcoal is my business, stranger.

FIRST PEASANT

They bring priest, doctor they still have no hope. He have a bad fever, and he cannot sweat.

MOUSTIQUE

And who is the man there, in the tall black hat. . . . Now
and at the hour of our death, amen.

FIRST PEASANT

He is Basil, the carpenter, and cabinet-maker. He going
down to hospital too, just in case . . . amen.

[A WOMAN *begins singing. A* SECOND PEASANT *comes
over*]

SECOND PEASANT

Who is he, what he want?

FIRST PEASANT

He say he hungry, and could we spare him some food?

[*The* WOMEN *have begun rubbing the* SICK MAN]

SECOND PEASANT

It have only enough for us here, brother.

[*The* WIFE *lets out a cry*]

MOUSTIQUE

Look, I know an old man, he been living in the forest, he
know all the herbs, plants, bush. He have this power and
glory, and if you want, and it have no harm in that, I
could fetch him for you. Look, before you pick him up
again, before you choke him with that stinking medicine,
before Basil the cabinet-maker get another job . . . Forever and ever, amen . . . Just something to eat and I will
go and fetch him. He don't want no money, but he could
cure this sick man.

SECOND PEASANT

How far he is?

MOUSTIQUE

Around the next bend, brother. All we ask is a little bread, a little piece of meat . . . for thine is the kingdom, the power and the glory . . .

FIRST PEASANT

I will ask his wife. Give him some bread. [*He goes over to the* WOMAN, *whispers, then returns*] All right. But if you . . . [*Goes for his cutlass*]

MOUSTIQUE

. . . At the hour of our death, amen.

[MOUSTIQUE *scuttles off. The women resume wailing, and the other men are about to raise the litter when the* FIRST PEASANT *stops them. Enter* MAKAK; *behind him,* MOUSTIQUE]

MOUSTIQUE

Here they are, Master. [*Hurriedly gesticulating, eating the bread, he removes his hat*] Here he is, my master. I have explain everything. Go ahead, master.

[MAKAK *enters, stands by the litter*]

MAKAK

Let all who want this man to heal, kneel down. I ask you. Kneel! [*They kneel, after some delay, except one or two men, whom* MOUSTIQUE *gently forces down*]

The man say kneel. Kneel!

MAKAK

Now I want a woman to put a coal in this hand, a living coal. A soul in my hand. [*He places one hand on the* SICK MAN's *forehead and holds out his palm. A* WOMAN *hesitantly places a coal in his palm.* MAKAK *winces, closing his eyes. We hear him groan, then silence*] We will wait for the moon.

[*A pause, then the full moon emerges slowly out of a cloud. We hear the dying man breathing hard*]

Like the cedars of Lebanon,
like the plantains of Zion,
the hand of God plant me
on Monkey Mountain.
He calleth to the humble.
And from that height
I see you all as trees,
like a twisted forest,
like trees without names,
a forest with no roots!
By this coal in my hand,
by this fire in my veins
let my tongue catch fire,
let my body, like Moses,
be a blazing bush.
Now sing in your darkness,

[*The* WOMEN *sing "Medelico"*]

sing out you forests,
and Josephus will sweat,
the sick man will dance,
sing as you sing
in the belly of the boat.
You are living coals,
you are trees under pressure,
you are brilliant diamonds
In the hand of your God.

[*They continue singing softly*]

Sweat, Josephus will sweat.
The fever will go!

[*They wait. Nothing happens*]

More coal. Hotter coal.
Sweat, Josephus, sweat.

[*They put more coals in his hand*]

And believe in me.
Faith, faith!
Believe in yourselves.

[*Silence*]

MOUSTIQUE

[*Furious at the failure, and frightened, he circulates among them, angrily*] Faith, faith! what happen to you? You didn't hear the man? You ain't hear the master. Sing, sing. Come on, Josephus, let that forehead shine, boy. Sing . . .

[*But the singing peters out.* MAKAK, *broken, moves away from the body. He looks at his dry palm*]

MAKAK

Let us go on, *compère*. These niggers too tired to believe anything again. Remember, is you all self that is your own enemy.

[*The* WIFE *comes forward with a gift of food, bread, vegetables, etc.*]

WIFE

I want to thank you, stranger. But what God want, nobody can change.

FIRST PEASANT

Come, come, put back on the medicine.

[*A* WOMAN *goes over to the pall and lets out a loud cry. The others turn. Laughing and weeping, she holds up her hand, which is wet from the* SICK MAN'S *brow*]

WOMAN

I'suait! I'suait! I'suait! I'suait! Sweat! He sweat!

[MAKAK *and* MOUSTIQUE *are apart, watching. The others rush up and in turn touch the freely sweating body and hold up their hand and rub their faces and taste the sweat, laughing and crying. One or two begin to dance. The* WIFE *bends over the man's body. The drummer and* CHORUS *join in the rhythm*]

ALL

I'suait! He sweat! *I'suait! Aie ya yie!*

[*The* CHORUS *picks up the sibilance. In the dancing and drumming to "Death, Oh Me Lord!"* MOUSTIQUE *takes over and, mounting a box, shouts above the celebration.* MAKAK, *dazed at his own power, is kneeling*]

MOUSTIQUE

Ah, ah, you see, all you.
Ain't white priest come and nothing happen?
Ain't white doctor come and was agony still?
Ain't you take bush medicine, and no sweat break?
White medicine, bush medicine,
not one of them work!
White prayers, black prayers,
and still no deliverance!
And who heal the man?
Makak! Makak!
All your deliverance lie in this man.
The man is God's messenger.
So, further the cause, brothers and sisters.

[*He opens his haversack and holds it before him*]

Further the cause,
drop what you have in there.
Look! Look! Josephus walking.
Next thing he will dance.

[*They laugh. The* WIFE *makes him do a little dance*]

I tell you he dancing!
God's work must be done,
and like Saint Peter self,
Moustique, that's me,
is Secretary-Treasurer.

[*During all this, they bring him gifts of food, some put money in the haversack, one man gives him the shoes he had slung around his neck*]

Now dance out in the moonlight,
let him breathe the fresh air,
let him breathe resurrection,
go forth, and rejoice . . .

> [*They take the* SICK MAN *out, dancing and singing
> "Death, Oh Me Lord!"* BASIL *hangs behind.* MOUSTIQUE
> *removes the tall hat from* BASIL *as he passes*]

MOUSTIQUE

You don't mind, friend? Only a black hat, in exchange for
a life. You see, the man heal, you ain't going to need it.

BASIL

My work never done, friend. And that hat is my business.

MOUSTIQUE

And mine, from now on.

BASIL

We go meet again, stranger.

MOUSTIQUE

Oh, I sure of that friend. But only at the sign of a spider.
[*He is counting the take in the hat*] Three coins, earrings.
Ah, a dollar. In God we trust. Like you, brother, I don't
believe in credit. Now, if you was a spider . . . The coat
too, pardner.

BASIL

You know where you are? [BASIL *surrenders the coat*]

MOUSTIQUE

At a crossroads in the moonlight.

BASIL

You are standing in the middle. A white road. With four legs. Think what that mean, friend. I can wait for my hat. [BASIL *exits*]

MOUSTIQUE

A white road. With four legs. A spider. With eggs. Eggs. White eggs! [*Shouting after* BASIL] But I still here! And I still alive! [*Laughing, he counts again.* MAKAK *comes towards him, mistaking him for* BASIL; *he stiffens*]

MAKAK

Moustique, Moustique. Oh, is you. You frighten me. What you doing there?

MOUSTIQUE

Counting. [*He continues*] And believe me, as the politician said, this better than working. Well, which way now, boss?

MAKAK

You see? You see what I do there? This power, this power I now have . . .

MOUSTIQUE

I see a sick man with snake bite, and a set o' damn asses using old-time medicine. I see a road paved with silver. I see the ocean multiplying with shillings. Thank God. That was good, that was good. [*Mimes the healing*] By this power in my hand. By this coal in my hand. You ain't playing you good, nuh. Here, take what you want.

MAKAK

[*Striking the hat away*] Move that from me. You don't understand, Moustique. This power I have, is not for profit.

MOUSTIQUE

[*Picking up the hat*] So what you want me to do? Run behind them and give them back their money? Look, I tired telling you that nothing is for free. That some day, Makak, swing high, swing low, you will have to sell your dream, your soul, your power, just for bread and shelter. That the love of people not enough, not enough to pay for being born, for being buried. Well, if you don't want the cash, then let me keep it. 'Cause I tired begging. Look, look at us. So poor we had to sell the donkey. Barefooted, nasty, and what you want me to do, bow my head and say thanks?

MAKAK

You will never understand. [MAKAK *kneels again*]

MOUSTIQUE

What you kneeling again for? Who you praying for now? [MAKAK *says nothing*] If is for me, partner, don't bother. Pray for the world to change. Not your friend. Pray for the day when people will not need money, when faith alone will move mountains. Pray for the day when poverty done, and for when niggers everywhere could walk upright like men. You think I doubt you, you think I don't respect you and love you and grateful to you? But I look at that moon, and it like a plate that a dog lick clean, bright as a florin, but dogs does chase me out of people yard when I go round begging, "Food for my master, food." And I does have to stoop down, and pick up the odd shilling they throw you. Look, turn your head, old man, look there, and that thing shining there, that is the ocean. Behind that, is Africa! How we going there? You think this . . . [*Holds up mask*] this damned stupidness go take us there? Either you let me save money for us, or here, at this crossroads, the partnership divide.

MAKAK

[*Rising*] All right, all right. But don't take more than we need. All right, which way now?

MOUSTIQUE

[*Spinning around blindly, he points*] This way, master. Quatre Chemin Market!

[*Music. Exeunt*]

Scene Three

[CORPORAL *in wig and gown enters the spotlight*]

CORPORAL

[*Infuriated*] My lords, behold! [*Arms extended*] Behold me, flayed and dismayed by this impenetrable ignorance! This is our reward, we who have borne the high torch of justice through tortuous thickets of darkness to illuminate with vision the mind of primeval peoples, of backbiting tribes! We who have borne with us the texts of the law, the Mosaic tablets, the splendours of marble in moonlight, the affidavit and the water toilet, this stubbornness and ingratitude is our reward! But let me not sway you with displays of emotion, for the law is emotionless. Let me give facts! [*He controls himself*] It was market Saturday and I, with Market and Sanitation Inspector Caiphas J. Pamphilion, was on duty at Quatre Chemin crossroads. I was armed because the area was on strike.

[*Sounds of the market: cries, etc., as the* MARKET SCENE, *baskets, cloth, etc., is lowered*]

A village market, at a crossroads, before dawn. Vendors, crates, carts, wares slung from rope. The FIRST VENDOR's cries, flute music. In one corner, setting up their basket-stall, a WOMAN, her HUSBAND, and two other VENDORS in near-rags, drinking coffee.

WIFE

He will tell you he see it, of course, but don't mind him, he wasn't there.

MAN

You was not there yourself. [*Piles the basket*]

WIFE

It was on the high road. The old woman husband Josephus, well, snake bite him, and they had called the priest and everything. From the edge of his bed he could see hell. Then Makak arrive—praise be God—and pass his hand so, twice over the man face, tell him to walk, and he rise up and he walk. And before that, he hold a piece of coal, so [*Demonstrates*], in his bare hand, open it, and the coal turn into a red bird, and fly out of his hand.

MAN

Hear her. [*Sucks his teeth*]

[*The market is waking around them, the light widening*]

WIFE

Then, the next day, this I cannot kiss the Bible that I see it myself, there had a small boy, he have, you know, a . . . a . . . what you call it?

MAN

Abscess.

257

WIFE

Right. A abscess. And he was in serious, serious pain, and the boy father bring him, and he rub a piece of bluestone on the boy . . . on the boy . . .

MAN

Cheek. By his cheek.

WIFE

Who telling the story, me or you? By the boy cheek, and the tooth fall out of the boy mouth, and he was well again. You want some more tea? [*She turns away*]

SECOND WOMAN

I hear that in Micoud he hold a stone in his hand and it turn into fire.

THIRD WOMAN

Not Micoud, it was by La Rivière.

SECOND WOMAN

Eh, bien. Wherever it was then.

MAN

[*To his wife*] *Gardez,* Agafa! is work you working or is talk you talking?

WIFE

What happen to you? You have no manners?

SECOND WOMAN

And for all that, he not asking for nothing.

THIRD WOMAN

They say it is a dream he have.

MAN

It have man so. It have men that have powers and nobody don't know where they getting it from. I did have a uncle so.

WIFE

If you did have a uncle so, you think is basket I would be selling? [*The* WOMEN *laugh*] It have more than a week now that thing happen with the man on the high road. Then the next day, the boy with the . . . with the . . .

SECOND WOMAN

Abscess.

WIFE

Whatever you calling it, at Micoud . . .

SECOND WOMAN

At La Rivière. He going to the sea, he must pass there.

[*The* CORPORAL, *wearing a pistol; and the* MARKET IN-SPECTOR, *issuing certificates to the* VENDORS]

INSPECTOR

So hence, the pistol?

CORPORAL

No, Market and Sanitary Inspector Pamphilion. *Mens sana in corpore sano.* The pistol is not to destroy but to protect.

You will ask me, to protect who from what, or rather, what from who? And my reply would be, to protect people from themselves, or, to put it another way, to preserve order for the people. We are in a state of emergency.

INSPECTOR

Is not because of the strikes and the cane-burning taking place in the district?

CORPORAL

No, Market Inspector Pamphilion, it is to prevent more strikes and cane-burning happening in the district. You understand?

INSPECTOR

No.

CORPORAL

Well, the law is complicated and people very simple. [*To a* VENDOR] Morning. That's a nice pawpaw, sir.

VENDOR

Oui, mon corporal. [*They move on*]

CORPORAL

You see?

INSPECTOR

That was a melon.

CORPORAL

I know. But in the opinion of the pistol, and for the preser-

vation of order, and to avoid any argument, we both was
satisfied it was a pawpaw.

INSPECTOR

I am beginning to understand the law.

CORPORAL

And if you know how much I would like to do for these
people, my people, you will understand even better. I
would like to see them challenge the law, to show me they
alive. But they paralyse with darkness. They paralyse with
faith. They cannot do nothing, because they born slaves
and they born tired. I could spit.

INSPECTOR

They must believe in something.

CORPORAL

Believe? Let me tell you what happen. I following this rumour good. And is the same as history, Pamphilion. Some
ignorant, illiterate lunatic who know two or three lines
from the Bible by heart, well one day he get tired of being
poor and sitting on his arse so he make up his mind to see
a vision, and once he make up his mind, the constipated,
stupid bastard bound to see it. So he come down off his
mountain, as if he is God self, and walk amongst the people, who too glad that he will think for them. He give them
hope, miracle, vision, paradise on earth, and is then blood
start to bleed and stone start to fly. And is at that point, to
protect them from disappointment, I does reach for my pistol. History, Mr. Pamphilion, is just one series of breach of

promise. [*They have reached the basket* VENDORS] That's a nice set of cages you have there.

VENDOR

Is a basket, Corporal.

CORPORAL

Good! I like a nigger with spirit.

WIFE

They say that he on a long walk, going through every village, on his way to the sea, looking across to Africa, and that when he get there, God will tell him what to do. [*She sings a hymn. The others join her, working*]

INSPECTOR

They know he is coming. The rumour like a cane fire. Faith is good business. I've never seen the market so full. It's like a fair. [*And indeed the market is filling with vendors, cripples, the sick*] From all parts of the district.

CORPORAL

The crippled, crippled. It's the crippled who believe in miracles. It's the slaves who believe in freedom.

INSPECTOR

And with music too! It's so beautiful I could cry, but I'm in uniform. My wife has rheumatism. I wonder.

[*In a corner of the market, an improvised music of sticks, clapping and a tin grater begins under the cries of the*

VENDORS. *Two men dance as another sings a bongo. The men mime a healing*]

SINGER
I'll show you how it happen: *Il dit Levez, Makak.* [He said Rise, Makak]

VENDOR
Pepper, pepperrrrr.

VENDOR
Plantainnnn!

DANCER
Woy, woy, Makak.

SINGER
Quittez charbon en sac. [Leave your bags of coal]

DANCER
Woy woy, Makak.

SINGER
Negre ka weh twop misere. [Niggers see too much misery]

VENDOR
Cassava, cassavaaah.

SINGER
Ous kai weh ou kai weh. [You'll see it for yourself]

DANCER
Woooh, Makak.

SINGER

Il dit Levez, Makak. [He said Wake up, Makak]

DANCER

Woiee, Makak.

SINGER

Il dit Descendre, Makak. [He said Come down, Makak]

DANCER

Woy, Makak.

SINGER

Descendre Morne Makak. [Go down Monkey Mountain] *Il dit . . .*

[*He stops, suddenly, as a small boy, a fishing pole in his hand, comes screaming into the market, huddles behind the* SINGER *and points. In the distance we hear the sound of a stick beating on a kerosene tin, and a voice roaring*]

SINGER

What happen? What happen, son?

BOY

I went down by the bridge by the river. I was looking in the water, down so, in the water, when I turn my head and . . . and I see a man alone singing and coming up the road, beating on a pan, and singing. With a long stick in his hand, and with a big white hair on his head, and . . . and a tall black hat, coming up the road so, one by one. I drop everything and I run like monson.

264

SINGER

C'est lui. C'est Makak.

CROWD

Makak. C'est Makak.

[*A woman screams.* MAKAK *enters leaping, whirling in black coat and tall hat and spear. This is in fact* MOUSTIQUE *impersonating* MAKAK]

MOUSTIQUE

Oui. C'est Makak.

CROWD

Makak, c'est Makak!

MOUSTIQUE

Oui. It is Makak.

[*Limping in his stride, he moves among the* CROWD]

Let the enemies of Africa make way.
Let the Abyssinian lion leap again,
For Makak walk in frenzy down Monkey Mountain,
And God send this message in lightning handwriting
That the sword of sunlight be in his right hand
And the moon his shield.

CORPORAL

You there!

MOUSTIQUE

Who it is dare to call Makak by name? Which man dare call the lion by his name?

CORPORAL

A corporal of police.

MOUSTIQUE

[*Turning to the* CROWD] I laugh. I laugh. A corporal of police? Makak have come to Quatre Chemin Market and neither corporal nor spiritual stopping him today! [*Pointing at the* CROWD] Dire, *Abou-ma-la-ka-jonga.*

CROWD

[*Defiantly*] *Abou-ma-la-ka-jonga.*

MOUSTIQUE

Faire ça. [*Gestures, with a stance*]

CROWD

Hunh. [*They gesture like him, many laughing*]

MOUSTIQUE

Now sing monkey! All you.

[*Sings*]

I don't know what to say that monkey won't do . . . Sing!

[WOMEN, *laughing, sing "monkey" as they strut around the* CORPORAL]

MOUSTIQUE

Take note, Corporal.

INSPECTOR

This is ignorance!

MOUSTIQUE

Ignorance? It seem to me I hear a voice, a voice, the colour
of milk, cry ignorance. [*Cups his ear. More laughter*] But
that voice is not the whispering of God who does pour counsel in the cup of great men ears, but just the usual voice of
small-time authority. What is your name?

INSPECTOR

I am Market Inspector Caiphas J. Pamphilion.

MOUSTIQUE

Market Inspector? Well then, inspect with respect, do not
be suspect, or you will be wreck. [*To* CROWD] They calling
that English, but the colour of English is white. Inspector of
milk! [*The* CROWD *is delirious*] Yes, find room in your heart
to laugh, find room inside you to be happy, because Makak
shall not pass this road again. His dream call him to the sea,
to the shore of Africa. And he hungry and tired. The dust of
thirty roads is in his throat. [*A woman brings him water*]
Daughter of heaven, Makak will remember you. But I prefer cash, as I travelling hard. Zambesi, Congo, Niger, Limpopo, is your brown milk I drink, is your taste I remember,
is the roots of your trees that is the veins in my hand, is your
flowers that falling now from my tongue. [*He takes the
bowl from the woman*] By belief, I make blessing. But even
the black sheep of God cannot go hungry. And they shall be
fed. So, children of darkness, bring what you can give, make
harvest and make sacrifice, bring whatsoever you have, a
shilling, a yam, and put here at the mouth of God, that
Makak is the tongue, and then, when all is in one bag, we
shall pray. You shall fast, and I shall pray. [*He lifts the bowl*

high above their heads as they place a few offerings at his feet] Kneel, and listen while I deliver the revelation of my experience. They say I can cure. Well, I cannot cure, except you want to be, except you believe that I can cure . . . Just put it down there, brother. Seven days and seven nights me and my friend, that great man, Moustique, who fall sick by the wayside, six days and six nights we leave Monkey Mountain, crossing hot pasture and dry river, like two leaves blowing in the hot wind. You will say how the divine sadness can fall on such men? A poor charcoal-seller that cannot see the light? *Eh bien,* listen, listen, Inspector of milk, and corporals of the law. One billion, trillion years of pressure bringing light, and is for that I say, Africa shall make light. And now . . . now . . . Makak shall sprinkle you with this water, for the cure is in yourself, and then, then he must go where his feet calling him. First, Makak will drink.

[*They look to him. He lifts the bowl reverently to his mouth, then drops it with a cry. He seems shaken*]

Is nothing. A spider. A spider over my hand. I cannot bear these things.

CORPORAL

A spider? A man who will bring you deliverance is afraid of a spider?

MOUSTIQUE

I not 'fraid of nothing. It just make me jump.

CORPORAL

Then show us. You. You, Basil, the carpenter, take it and bring it for the warrior Makak. Take it.

> [BASIL *looks for the spider, holds it in his cupped palm and brings it towards* MAKAK *and places it on his body.* MAKAK *winces, enduring it. Shuddering*]

BASIL

[*As he gets nearer, looks into his eyes*] You cannot run fast enough, eh? Moustique! That is not Makak! His name is Moustique!

MOUSTIQUE

Eh?

> [*A man comes nearer.* MOUSTIQUE, *for that is who it is, stares at him, sweating.* BASIL *steps forward*]

LABOURER

Wait! Wait! It is Basil the carpenter. Let him speak.

> [*A rustling stillness*]

BASIL

I have little to say. Why should I talk? Look for yourselves. The tongue is on fire, but the eyes are dead.

> [MOUSTIQUE *cowers, mumbling.* BASIL, *sometimes moving the spider around* MOUSTIQUE's *body, circles him, talking slowly, slowly waving his arms. During this, he removes the silk hat*]

You have seen coals put out by water. What comes from that mouth is vapour, steam, promises without meaning.

The eyes are dead coals. [*The* CROWD *mutters*] And the heart is ashes. [*He confronts* MOUSTIQUE] Ah, friend, when the spear of moonlight had pinned the white road till its legs were splayed like a spider [*He opens one palm*], I tried to direct you. Everywhere you were shown signs. In the hut that first morning, in the white shrieking of the funeral procession, in the mask of the cold moon, but you would not listen.

MOUSTIQUE

Who in hell is he? What he want? What he want?

BASIL

I want nothing, pardner. And I go get it. You have one chance! If this is Makak, if this man will deliver the revelation of his experience, then let him show you your hope! Ask him to share it with you! Show them! Show them what you have learnt, *compère!*

CROWD

Yes! Show us! Show us!

CORPORAL

[*Shouting*] What is your name? Your name not Moustique?

CROWD

Show us! Show us!

MOUSTIQUE

[*Pushing* BASIL *aside*] You know who I am? You want to know who I am? Makak! Makak! or Moustique, is not the

270

same nigger? What you want me to say? "I am the resurrection, I am the life"? "I am the green side of Jordan," or that "I am a prophet stoned by Jerusalem," or you all want me, as if this hand hold magic, to stretch it and like a flash of lightning to make you all white? God after god you change, promise after promise you believe, and you still covered with dirt; so why not believe me. All I have is this [*Shows the mask*], black faces, white masks! I tried like you. Moustique then! Moustique! [*Spits at them*] That is my name! Do what you want!

LABOURER

And you come here to rob your own people? What is one more mosquito? What is one more man?

MOUSTIQUE

Die in your ignorance! Live in darkness still! You don't know what you want!

[CROWD *grows angrier*]

LABOURER

Well then take that from us! [*Clouts him.* MOUSTIQUE *falls*]

CROWD

Kill him! Break his legs! Beat him! Kill him!

[*They beat him to a noise of sticks rattling, tins banging and screaming women. The* CORPORAL *stands apart, then he moves towards them*]

CORPORAL

All right, all right! *Assez, assez!* I say enough. Go home. Go home before I arrest all of you. Go home!

[*They disperse, leaving* MOUSTIQUE *crumpled among the heap of offerings.* BASIL *picks up his hat, puts it on, then waits*]

INSPECTOR

Why you didn't stop them?

CORPORAL

All those people. Do you want me to get killed? Come on. I'll buy you a drink. You look afraid. Funny, I can't stand cockroaches myself.

INSPECTOR

It was a spider. Harmless.

CORPORAL

Well, whatever it was. Come on, let's go.

[MAKAK, *dusty and tattered, enters the market*]

MAKAK

Moustique? Moustique? [*He looks around, among the wreckage, and then discovers* MOUSTIQUE, *sprawled on a heap*] Moustique. What happen? What happen to you? What they do you? [*He lifts up* MOUSTIQUE's *head*] Oh God, what they do you, little man?

MOUSTIQUE

Pardon, Makak. Pardon. To see that this is where I must die. Here, in the market. The spider, the spider. [*He shudders*] Go back to Monkey Mountain. Go back, or you will die like this.

MAKAK

You will not die.

MOUSTIQUE

Yes, I will die. I take what you had, I take the dream you have and I come and try to sell it. I try to fool them, and they fall on me with sticks, everything, and they kill me.

MAKAK

How you could leave me alone, Moustique? In all the yards and villages I pass, I hear people saying, Makak was here, Makak was here, and we give him so and so. If it was for the money, I didn't know.

MOUSTIQUE

No. You didn't know. You would never know. It was always me, since the first time in the road, where . . . always me who did have to beg . . . to do . . . [*He passes out.* MAKAK *shakes him*]

MAKAK

Moustique, Moustique.

MOUSTIQUE

Go back, go back to Monkey Mountain. Go back.

MAKAK

No, she tell me what I must do.

MOUSTIQUE

Let me die, Makak, I hurting and I tired, tired . . .

273

MAKAK

You will not die, you must not die!

MOUSTIQUE

Every man have to die . . . [*He faints again.* MAKAK *shakes him*]

MAKAK

Then look. Look then . . . Open your eyes, try and open your eyes, and tell me what you see. Look, look, then, if you dying, tell me what you see. Open them. Tell me and I will preach that. Tell me!

MOUSTIQUE

I see . . . I see . . . I see a black wind blowing . . . A black wind . . . [*He dies*]

MAKAK

[*Forcing his eyes open*] And nothing else? Nothing? Let me look in them, let me look, and I will keep the last picture of your eyes in mine, let me be brave and look in a dead man eye, Moustique . . . [*He peers into* MOUSTIQUE'S *gaze and what he sees there darkens his vision. He lets out a terrible cry of emptiness*]

MAKAK

Aiieeeeee. Moustique!

[*In the darkness the drums begin, and shapes, demons, spirits, a cleft-footed woman, a man with a goat's head, imps, whirl out of the darkness around* MAKAK, *and the*

*figure of a woman with a white face and long black hair
of the mask, all singing. They take the body on a litter]*

CHORUS

Death, O death, O me Lord,
When my body lie down in the grave,
Then me soul going shout for joy.

[To a frenzied climax as MAKAK *writhes on the ground
in a fit, and the music dies]*

Part Two

Let us add, for certain other carefully selected unfortunates, that other witchery of which I have already spoken: Western culture. If I were them, you may say, I'd prefer my mumbo-jumbo to their Acropolis. Very good: you've grasped the situation. But not altogether, because you aren't them—or not yet. Otherwise you would know 'hat they can't choose; they must have both. Two worlds; that makes two bewitchings; they dance all night and at dawn they crowd into the churches to hear Mass; each day the split widens. Our enemy betrays his brothers and becomes our accomplice; his brothers do the same thing. The status of "native" is a nervous condition introduced and maintained by the settler among colonised people with their consent.

Sartre: Introduction to "The Wretched of the Earth," by Frantz Fanon

Scene One

The cell. Night. TIGRE and SOURIS in their cell. MAKAK in his. The
CORPORAL enters, banging a tin plate with a cup.

CORPORAL

All right, all right! Chow-time! Stand back. Up against the
bars there! I ain't want you all chewing up my hand for
three green figs and a sliver of salfish. Hold this plate. [TIGRE
steps forward, accepts plate, steps back] You next. [SOURIS
steps forward, accepts plate and cup, then steps back] How
is the old king?

SOURIS

He's been there moaning, muttering to himself, since he
come in. Sometimes he sing, sometimes he letting out a
cry, sometimes even a little dance, and half the time in
gibberish. One more green fig, Corporal?

CORPORAL

No more figs. Any more you get will have to be in your
mind. A figment of your imagination, so to speak.

SOURIS

Look at him. Just look at him. I feel sorry for him. Let him go, Corporal.

CORPORAL

I am an instrument of the law, Souris. I got the white man work to do. Besides, if he crazy he dangerous. If he is not, a night in jail will be good for his soul. [*Goes over to the old man's cell*] Is chow time, King-Kong. Hey. Food, food, old man.

TIGRE

Bring me damn supper, Lestrade! I have me rights, you know!

CORPORAL

Your rights? Listen, nigger! according to this world you have the inalienable right to life, liberty, and three green figs. No more, maybe less. You can do what you want with your life, you can hardly call this liberty, and as for the pursuit of happiness, you never hear the expression, give a nigger an inch and he'll take a mile? Don't harass me further. I didn't make the rules. [*To* MAKAK] Now, you. Come for this plate!

[MAKAK *gropes forward*]

TIGRE

So what? Is against the law to be poor?

CORPORAL

Here, hold this. [*Turns to* TIGRE] Don't tell me about the law. Once I loved the law. I thought the law was just, universal, a substitute for God, but the law is a whore, she will adjust her price. In some places the law does not allow you to be black, not even black, but tinged with black.

TIGRE

And that is what eating out your soul, Lestrade. That is why you punishing this man. You punishing your own grandfather. Let him go home.

MAKAK

Let me go home. I will pay you. I have money. I have money that I hide . . . all of you.

CORPORAL

Bribery! [*Pulling the old man through the bars*] Listen, you corrupt, obscene, insufferable ape, I am incorruptible, you understand? Incorruptible. The law is your salvation and mine, you imbecile, you understand that. This ain't the bush. This ain't Africa. This is not another easy-going nigger you talking to, but an officer! A servant and an officer of the law! Not the law of the jungle, but something the white man teach you to be thankful for.

MAKAK

It is the law that kill my friend. You let them kill my friend.

CORPORAL

I don't know what you talking about.

MAKAK

You lie . . . You lie. Right here, in the market . . . you let them kill my friend.

SOURIS

My figs, Corporal, my figs!

CORPORAL

Shut up! Shut up, nigger!

SOURIS

[*Dancing*] O you beast! You filt'y fascist beast! I hungry!

MAKAK

I will give you all the money I have to go back home. O Moustique, you did warn me. I open my eyes and I see nothing. I see man quarrelling like animals in a pit. The spider there for all of us. I see us in this pit . . .

CORPORAL

How long he been like this?

TIGRE

Since you bring him in. After the first fit. Is like he is living over and over a bad dream he had.

SOURIS

I hungreeeeeeeeeee!

CORPORAL

All right! All right! The law says I must feed you. I will feed you. But God, remind me to ask for a transfer to civilization. [*Exit*]

TIGRE

[*In a single spot*] You hear what he say? Ain't I tell you old men so does have money hide away. We must help the old bitch escape, track him to Monkey Mountain, then put him out of his misery. Eat your food when it come, but dream about money, Souris. Dream hard and good. Shhhhhh.

TIGRE

Tell us about the money. About that . . . and Africa.

MAKAK

You will laugh at me.

SOURIS

Where is it?

TIGRE

We believe your dream, Makak. Tell us . . . and . . . look . . . You want to get out of here?

MAKAK

Yes, yes, but how?

TIGRE

Never mind how. You want to get out?

MAKAK

[*Wearily*] Yes . . .

TIGRE

Listen. First we must kill the Corporal.

SOURIS

I know now you crazy.

TIGRE

You know why you must kill him? Because she tell you to, old man, remember, in the dream? Lion, she call you. And lion don't stop to think. The jaw of the lion, that is the opening and closing of the book of judgement. When the moon in quarter, you know what Africans say . . .

SOURIS

Where you get all that?

MAKAK

Tell me, my son, what?

TIGRE

That the jaw of the sun, that is the lion, has eaten the moon. The moon, that is nothing, but . . . a skull . . . a bone . . .

[MAKAK, *growling, begins to pace his cage*]

SOURIS

Pappy! Eh?

TIGRE

How else can you prove your name is lion, unless you do one bloody, golden, dazzling thing, eh? And who stand in your way but your dear friend, Corporal Lestrade the straddler, neither one thing nor the next, neither milk, coal, neither day nor night, neither lion nor monkey, but a mulatto, a foot-licking servant of marble law? He cause Moustique to die. He turn his back on that. Believe me, like your friend saw the spider, I see it clearly. You bastard son of a black gorilla, you listening?

SOURIS

Look, look, he standing still.

TIGRE

He have something in his hand.

SOURIS

The same mask again.

TIGRE

No. No . . . friend . . . As the moon unsheathe its blade, I swear by the crucifix of the handle, the old black gentleman has unclouded . . .

SOURIS

[*In wonder*] A knife!

TIGRE

Look how it shines, old man. Like the sea. Like silver. Think of the bright blood! Think like the lion that is dazzled by pity for only a second! Call the Corporal . . . Then, when the moon come out again, pretend you going mad . . . Yes. You are in the forest now, you are hunted, tired. Your heavy, hanging tongue is dry as sand. Your muscles thunder with exhaustion. You want to drink. Fall down, ask for water . . . a drink . . . Pretend you catch a fit. And then the keys, the keys! [*Loudly*] Corporal! Corporal! Shhhhhh . . . Go back to sleep . . . Corporal!

[CORPORAL *enters with a red towel, wiping his hands*]

CORPORAL

What you want, Tigre?

TIGRE

I cannot sleep . . . I . . . I thirsty . . . And the old man over there, groaning and coughing like a sick lion all night . . . Between him and the moon they keeping me up. The night hot like a forest fire. He must be thirsty too.

[*The* CORPORAL *comes to* MAKAK'*s cell*]

CORPORAL

Old man . . . you thirsty? [*He goes nearer*]

TIGRE

For blood, perhaps. Not you who call him lion?

CORPORAL

He who? that ape? What you want to drink, old man . . .

MAKAK

[*With a cry*] Blood! Blood! Blood! Lion . . . Lion . . . I am . . . a lion [*He has grabbed the* CORPORAL, *stabbing him. Then he hurls him to the floor*]

TIGRE

The keys! The keys!

[MAKAK *takes the keys and opens the cells*]

MAKAK

[*Holding* TIGRE *and* SOURIS *and near-weeping with rage*]

Drink it! Drink it! Drink! Is not that they say we are? Animals! Apes without law? O God, O gods! What am I, I who thought I was a man? What have I done? Which God? God dead, and his law there bleeding. Christian, cannibal, I will drink blood. You will drink it with me. For the lion, and the tiger, and the rat, yes, the gentle rat, have come out of their cages to breathe the air, the air heavy with forest, and if that moon go out . . . I will still find my way; the blackness will swallow me. I will wear it like a fish wears water . . . Come. You have tasted blood. Now, come!

TIGRE

Where? To Monkey Mountain?

MAKAK

[*Laughing*] Come! [*Looks at body*]

[*They exit*]

CORPORAL

[*Clutching the towel to his wound, rises. Single spot*] Did you feel pity for me or horror of them? Believe me, I am all right. Only a flesh wound. Times change, don't they? and people change. Even black people, even slaves. He made his point, you might say. [*Drawing out a knife*] But this is only what they dream of. And before things grow clearer, nearer to their dream of revenge, I must play another part. We'll go hunting the lion. Except . . . [*Takes down a rifle*] . . . They're not lions, just natives. There's nothing quite so exciting as putting down the natives. Especially after reason and law have failed. So I let them

286

escape. Let them run ahead. Then I'll have good reason for shooting them down. Sharpeville? Attempting to escape. Attempting to escape. Attempting to escape from the prison of their lives. That's the most dangerous crime. It brings about revolution. So, off we go, lads! [*Drums. Exit chanting*]

Scene Two

The forest. Enter MAKAK, SOURIS, TIGRE.

MAKAK

Come, we will rest here. I know this forest. Smell it. Smell it, it speaks to your blood.

SOURIS

Yes, it saying, your damn foot bleeding. It saying, "You hungry?" And the answer is yes. You know where we are, in all this damn darkness?

MAKAK

I can read the palm of every leaf. I can prophesy from one crystal of dew.

SOURIS

Good! Then read what we having for supper.

MAKAK

I know the nature of fire and wind. I will make a small fire. Here, look, you see this plant? Dry it, fire it, and your mind will cloud with a sweet, sweet-smelling smoke. Then the smoke will clear. You will not need to eat.

TIGRE

You crazy ganga-eating bastard, I want meat. Flesh and blood. Wet grass. Come on, come on, show us the way to Monkey Mountain. The Corporal hunting us.

MAKAK

The first quality of animals is stillness. Keep still. I can hear the crack of every leaf. I know all the signals of insects. It will be a small fire. [*He moves off*]

TIGRE

Come on, come on, old man. We have to reach Monkey Mountain.

MAKAK

Monkey Mountain?

TIGRE

I . . . I mean Africa.

SOURIS

We should 'a eat first, then killed the Corporal. [*Whispers*] You really think he have money? Look at him! Half-man, half-forest, a shadow moving through the leaves.

TIGRE

Just do as he say. That's all. This is his forest. He could easily lose us. You didn't see how he stabbed the Corporal? He coming back. Let's mix ourselves in his madness. Let's dissolve in his dream. [*As* MAKAK *returns with twigs, bush, etc.*] Ah, Africa! Ah, blessed Africa! Whose earth is a starved mother waiting for the kiss of her prodigal, for the kiss of my foot. Talk like that, you fool.

SOURIS

How you will take us to Africa? What we will do there? In the darkness, now that I can see nothing, maybe, it is there I am. When I was a little boy, living in darkness, I was so afraid, it was as if I was sinking, drowning in a grave, and me and the darkness was the same, and God was like a big white man, a big white man I was afraid of.

MAKAK

Here, you are at home, my son. One of the forest creatures.

SOURIS

And in the darkness, big man as I am, I still afraid of him. You 'fraid God, Tigre?

TIGRE

I not 'fraid no white man.

SOURIS

Well, God help us. I really frighten. Like a child again. [MAKAK *lights the fire. They watch him*] And that is what they teach me since I small. To be black like coal, and to dream of milk. To love God, and obey the white man.

TIGRE

[*Whispering*] Enough! Enough! You going crazy too?

SOURIS

How we will go, old man? How we will go?

MAKAK

Once, when Moustique asked me that, I didn't know. But
I know now. What power can crawl on the bottom of the
sea, or swim in the ocean of air above us? The mind, the
mind. Now, come with me, the mind can bring the dead
to life, it can go back, back, back, deep into time. It can
make a man a king, it can make him a beast. Can you hear
the sea now, can you hear the sound of suffering, we are
moving back now . . . [*The* CHORUS *chants, "I going
home"*] Back into the boat, a beautiful boat, and soon,
after many moons, after many songs, we will see Africa, the
golden sand, the rivers where lions come down to drink,
lapping at the water with their red tongues, then the villages, the birds, the sound of flutes.

SOURIS

Yes, yes, I see it. I see it!

MAKAK

When your eyes open, you will be transformed, as if you
have eaten a magic root.

[SOURIS *moves off*]

TIGRE

We will need money to go there, uncle. To buy a boat. A
big, big boat that will take everybody back, or otherwise,
is back into jail. Back where we were! It's drizzling. Where
Souris gone? Where that damn thief? Is drizzling and I
cold. And the light of the coals making figures in the
forest. The trees take one step nearer. The leaves are eyes
and tongues. And there are eyes or diamonds winking in

the bush. Old man, if I go with you, what will I find? If they don't hang us for killing the Corporal.

MAKAK

Look at those coals. When I look in the fire, I see visions. The fire will talk with its bright tongue. Tell me what you see?

TIGRE

[*Huddled, shivering*] I see hell. I see people black like coals, twisting and burning in hell. And I see me too. The rain will put it out. Where Souris? I hungry. By tomorrow they will catch us, and three of us will hang. *Tiens*, what is that? But you, they will let you go, because you old, ugly and crazy. Where that mouse? Where that damn Souris? What I will find in Africa?

MAKAK

Peace.

TIGRE

Peace? Piece of what? [*The squawk of an animal*] What was that? What in hell is happening? Where Souris gone? For the first time in my life, I feeling frighten. Come, come on, you old bastard, let us move on.

MAKAK

[*Suddenly grabbing him*] Then, when we get there, I will make you my general. General Tigre, and when my enemies come, I will say fight with him, because he is a man, a man who know how to hate, to whom the life of a man is

292

like a mosquito, like a fly. [*Claps his hands at an insect, and drops it in the fire.* TIGRE *laughs*] And the fire is up to God.

[SOURIS *enters, holding up a dead chicken*]

SOURIS

Well then, God best keep the fire going, 'cause look what drop in through the garden. [*Drops chicken*] And then, ay, what is this, what is this? [*Feels around in his large coat*] O Blessed Saviour, a miracle. Ground provisions, look, potatoes, one yam, never take more than you need, for the Lord will provide, a hand of small onions, and a little pepper. [*Spills them onto the ground*] So, how is the king?

[MAKAK *has drawn apart, talking to himself*]

TIGRE

Mad like a ant. He just make me general.

MAKAK

[*Trotting up to them*] Good, my men. Good, my men. The Lord on the day he dead [*Opening his arms*] had two thief by him.

SOURIS

Only one went in heaven. [*Plucking the chicken*]

TIGRE

You. Because I look in the fire, and I see myself burning there, forever and forever, amen.

SOURIS

Amen. [MAKAK *walks away again, regally, mumbling*] So what we will do with him?

TIGRE

Let us eat first. I will peel the yams. [*He takes out a knife and they watch* MAKAK *as they work*]

SOURIS

Mad, mad, mad.

TIGRE

You see his eyes? That is the eyes of a man who will kill you in your sleep. They looking at you, and like you not there. Once we letting him believe what he is, is all right. Otherwise . . . [*Draws the knife across his throat*] Look, his blanket fall off.

SOURIS

I will fix it.

> [MAKAK *has sat down on a log.* SOURIS *gingerly goes up to the fallen blanket and places it around the old man's shoulders*]

MAKAK

My crown.

SOURIS

[*Twisting a vine and crowning him*] Crown. And don't bother call me for your sword, until the damn yams boil.

MAKAK

[*In a thundering voice*] Feed my armies!

SOURIS

Pardon?

MAKAK

Feed my armies! Look, look them there. [*Rises and gestures beyond the fire*] They waiting for their general, their king, Makak, to tell them when to eat. Salute them. You see them where they are? Salute them. Let my generals salute them. Like me.

TIGRE

Salute, Couillon. [SOURIS *salutes*]

MAKAK

General Tigre?

TIGRE

Look me, general. [*Rises, salutes*]

MAKAK

Attention, and listen. I want to speak to my men. I want to tell my armies, you can see their helmets shining like fireflies, you can see their spears as thick as bamboo leaves. I want to tell them this. That now is the time, the time of war. War. Fire, fire and destruction. [*He takes his spear and dips it in the fire*] Fire, death. [SOURIS *and* TIGRE *withdraw in the darkness, and the sky grows red*] Fire. The sky is on fire. Makak will destroy.

SOURIS

[*Still saluting*] *Eh, bien.* We reach Africa.

MAKAK

Shh! Somebody coming. The fire! Come. Into the bushes! Shh! Somebody coming.

[*Enter the* CORPORAL *armed, alone*]

CORPORAL

Ho! Ho! My beaters, ho! My head. My wound. Dusty blade.
Gangrene. Delirium! Thrash that bush there! Build a fire
for my safari. Set down the white man's burden. My back
is breaking. Whisky and soda, you smoke-black sod. And
start smoking out the mosquitoes. Bwana Lestrade is tired.
Once I knew this jungle like the black of my hand.
What-ho, chaps, more lights. Come dawn like thunder and
we'll blow their brains out. [*He kneels down beside the
fire*] Ah! Ashes! Ashes and naked footprints! Black footprints. Let me stalk and think. Aha! Oho! Over here! Over
here, bring me my Mannlicher, then a gimlet. [*Looking
down*] Uh-huh. Footpad of tiger, ferrule of rat, spoor of
lion, and all leading up the garden path to . . . [*Looking
up*] To Monkey Mountain.

[*Wild cackling laughter*]

Gibberish! No fear, lads! Steady on! A calm blue eye acquired this Empire. Mine, a tawny yellow. English! You
animals! English! English!

[*More laughter, coughs, howls*]

Animals! Savages! [*Quietly*] My wound! I'll pack my wound
with earth! Niggers? God, the fire's gone out, lads! The
light of civilization's finished. M'tbutu! Zola! Who's there?
The moon, the moon, the pock-marked moon alone, the
siphylitic crone. Who's that?

[*In the moonlight,* BASIL *comes out of the bushes*]

Who are you? I'm going mad, goddammit. Stiff upper lip.

Who're you in that ridiculous gear? Shoot! Or I'll stop!
Stop or I'll run. It's Basil, is it? Time up. Twilight of Empire, eh? Night of the what's what? Who in hell are you?
Qui moune? [BASIL *waits, his face hidden*] You speak Swa-
hili? Creole? Papiamento? Urdu? Ibo? Who you?

BASIL

I am Basil, the carpenter, the charcoal seller. I do not exist.
A figment of the imagination, a banana of the mind . . .

CORPORAL

Banana of the mind, figment of the . . . ho! That's pretty
good. Goodbye. [*He goes*]

BASIL

You have one minute to repent. To recant. To renounce.

CORPORAL

Repent? Renounce what?

BASIL

You know, Lestrade. You know.

[TIGRE *and* SOURIS *emerge*]

CORPORAL

My mind, my mind. What's happened to my mind?

BASIL

It was never yours, Lestrade.

CORPORAL

Then if it's not mine, then I'm not mad.

BASIL

And if you are not mad, then all this is real.

CORPORAL

Impossible! There is Monkey Mountain. Here is the earth.
Banana of the mind . . . ha . . . ha . . . ha . . .

TIGRE

What happen to him? What he looking at?

SOURIS

I don't know, but he look crazy. It must be the wound. Or
. . . Is the moon. Is the moon . . .

BASIL

Confess your sins, Lestrade. Confess your sins. Strip yourself naked. Look at your skin and confess your sins.

CORPORAL

Which sins? What sins?

TIGRE

[*Stepping nearer*] At the edge of death you'll remember
them. Confess!

CORPORAL

[*As the creatures circle him*] Mooma, don't cry, your son in
the grave already. Our son in the grave already, Mooma,
don't cry . . . But he's crying, Mother. Mother India,
Mother Africa, Mother Earth, he is crying. Why? Why?
[*Tries to sing*] "By the light of the silvery moon." [*Weeps*]

Whistle, boys, it's only death. [*Whistles weakly*] The earth, the earth was a black child holding a balloon, and somebody cut it.

BASIL

Fifteen seconds.

TIGRE

Who de hell he talking to? I see nothing.

SOURIS

I see nothing too.

MAKAK

He is talking to nothing.

BASIL

Ten seconds.

CORPORAL

[*Flatly, like an accustomed prayer*] All right. Too late have I loved thee, Africa of my mind, *sero te amavi*, to cite Saint Augustine who they say was black. I jeered thee because I hated half of myself, my eclipse. But now in the heart of the forest at the foot of Monkey Mountain [*The creatures withdraw*] I kiss your foot, O Monkey Mountain. [*He removes his clothes*] I return to this earth, my mother. Naked, trying very hard not to weep in the dust. I was what I am, but now I am myself. [*Rises*] Now I feel better. Now I see a new light. I sing the glories of Makak! The glories of my race! What race? I have no race! Come! Come, all you splendours of imagination. Let me sing of darkness now! My hands. My hands are heavy. My feet . . . [*He rises, crouched*] My feet grip like roots. The arteries are like rope. [*He howls*] Was that my voice? My voice. O God, I have become what I mocked. I always was, I always was. Makak! Makak! forgive me, old father.

MAKAK

[*Stepping forward*] Now he is one of us.

CORPORAL

[*Looking up*] Grandfather. Grandfather. Where am I? Where is this? Why am I naked?

MAKAK

Because like all men you were born here. Here, put this around you. [*He covers him with the sack*] What is this?

CORPORAL

A gun.

MAKAK

We don't need this, do we?

[TIGRE *and* SOURIS *approach cautiously*]

They reject half of you. We accept all. Rise. Take off your boots. Doesn't the floor of the forest feel cool under your foot? Don't you hear your own voice in the gibberish of the leaves? Look how the trees have opened their arms. And in the hoarseness of the rivers, don't you hear the advice of all our ancestors. When the moon is hidden, look how you sink, forgotten, into the night. The forest claims us all, my son. No one needs gloves in his grave.

TIGRE

Tie up the bastard and let him find his way back.

SOURIS

So how it feel to be a nigger, Corporal? Animals. Savages! Niggers! Stop turning the place into a stinking zoo! [*Hops around*] Who is the monkey now, Lestrade? You bitch! I long had this for you. [*Jumps on him, wrestling*] And this! And this!

MAKAK

Enough! You hearing me? Enough! I came unto my own and they turned me away. Fighting, squabbling among yourselves. I have brought a dream to my people, and they rejected me. Now they must be taught, even tortured, killed. Their skulls will hang from my palaces. I will break up their tribes.

TIGRE

[*Picking up the rifle*] All right. Up till now I been playing this game. Shadows and shapes been crossing my mind, I have felt my body altered by firelight, and I watched all three of you, like animals paralysed by the glare of a headlamp. About three miles back there is Quatre Chemin jail, remember that, Souris, is where you and I come from. Up there is the damn mountain, I don't know if you have money, uncle, but I intend to find out. [*Cocks trigger*]

Come on now, move! Souris, get the Corporal belt, and tie
up his hands. Souris! You ent hear me?

SOURIS

No, Tigre.

TIGRE

What happen to you? You know who talking to you? You
know what you are? Don't make me have to shoot.

SOURIS

You can't shoot us all, Tigre.

TIGRE

Whose side you on, nigger?

SOURIS

I believe this old man.

TIGRE

What the hell you talking about?

SOURIS

I believe I am better than I am. He teach me that. [*Picks
up a rock*] Now you know me, Tigre. You will have to
shoot.

TIGRE

You know what you saying? You going break up our friendship for one worthless, lunatic old charcoal-burner?

SOURIS

He teach me more than you ever teach me, Tigre. His madness worth more to me than your friendship. Are you sure where you are, Tigre, are you sure who you are?

TIGRE

I'm a criminal with a gun, in the heart of the forest under Monkey Mountain. And I want his money.

MAKAK

Money . . . That is what you wanted? That is what it is all about . . . money . . . ?

TIGRE

Shut up! Africa, Monkey Mountain, whatever you want to call it. But you first, father, to where the money buried. Go on. You too, Lestrade. Walk.

MAKAK

[*Moves forward, then stops*] I am lost. I have forgotten the way. Who are you?

TIGRE

My name is Tigre.

MAKAK

But you, like him, had your own dream of money. The tiger eats and lies down content, but tomorrow he must rise again. Think, Tigre, money is not what you want. I know now you cannot reach that rainbow weighted like scales with your bags of fool's gold, no more than I can ever reach that moon; and that is why I am lost.

SOURIS

You will bring us so far, then abandon us? You will surrender that dream?

MAKAK

[*Holding out the mask*] I was a king among shadows. Either the shadows were real, and I was no king, or it is my own kingliness that created the shadows. Either way, I am lonely, lost, an old man again. No more. I wanted to leave this world. But if the moon is earth's friend, eh, Tigre, how can we leave the earth. And the earth, self. Look down and there is nothing at our feet. We are wrapped in black air, we are black, ourselves shadows in the firelight of the white man's mind. Soon, soon it will be morning, praise God, and the dream will rise like vapour, the shadows will be real, you will be corporal again, you will be thieves, and I an old man, drunk and disorderly, beaten down by a Bible, and tired of looking up to heaven. You believe I am lost now? Shoot, go ahead and shoot me. Death is the last shadow I have made. The Carpenter is waiting.

[BASIL *waits in the shadows*]

SOURIS

But your dream touch everyone, sir. Even in those burnt-out coals of your eyes, there is still some fire. Dying, but fire. If a wind could catch them again, if some wind, some breath. [*He looks into his eyes*]

MAKAK

And these tears will put them out. I have left death, fail-
ure, disappointment, despair in the wake of my dreams.
[*The* CORPORAL *has picked up* MAKAK'S *spear. He faces*
TIGRE]

[*A dance begins*]

The tribes! The tribes will wrangle among themselves,
spitting, writhing, hissing, like snakes in a pit.

CORPORAL

I seen death face to face, Tigre, look! He's behind you.
Turn, and he turns with you!

TIGRE

You turn savage, red nigger?

SOURIS

Stop them, stop them. [*They are circling each other*]

MAKAK

Locked in a dream, and treading their own darkness. Snarl-
ing at their shadows, snapping at their own tails, devour-
ing their own entrails like the hyena, eaten with self-hatred.
O God, O gods, why did you give me this burden?

SOURIS

For God sake, Tigre!

CORPORAL

Look, he's behind you!

TIGRE

Ha, ha, there's nothing behind me.

BASIL

Tigre! [TIGRE *turns. The* CORPORAL *leaps onto him with a cry and drives the spear through him*]

MAKAK

[*Over* TIGRE's *body*] The tribes! The tribes! One by one, they will be broken. One will sink, and the other rise, like the gold and silver scales of the sun and the moon, and that is named progress.

CORPORAL

Now we must press on, old man. He is out of the way. This is jungle law. Come on, come on.

MAKAK

Yes, but where?

CORPORAL

Where? Anywhere! Onward, onward. Progress. Press on. We need that cry, and those who do not bend to our will, to your will, must die. You, help him up.

SOURIS

He doesn't know where to go.

CORPORAL

Put him in front. He's a shadow now. Let him face the moon and move towards it. Let him go forward. I'll take

over. Come on. Go. Drag that thing there into the bush.
[SOURIS *takes away* TIGRE's *body and* BASIL *helps him*] Now,
where to, old father? No. We cannot go back. History is in
motion. The law is in motion. Forward, forward.

SOURIS

Where? The world is a circle, Corporal. Remember that.

[*They move off, wearily. The* CORPORAL *remains behind
in a single spot*]

CORPORAL

Bastard, hatchet-man, opportunist, executioner. I have the
black man work to do, you know. I breathe over the shoulder of your leaders, I hang back always at a decent distance,
but I am there to observe that the law is upheld, that those
who break it, president or prince, will also be broken. I
have no ambition of my own. I have no animal's name. I
simply work. And if a niche in history opens for me, what
else can I do, for the sake of the people, Vox Populi, but
to step into it? I don't know where we are going. But forward, progress! When you reach the precipice, simply step
aside. That right, Basil? You see, he is not here. Now, let
splendour, barbarism, majesty, noise, slogans, parades,
drown out that truth. Plaster the walls with pictures of the
leader, magnify our shadows, moon, if only for a moment.
Gongs, warriors, bronzes! Statues, clap your hands you
forests. Makak will be enthroned!

Scene Three

Apotheosis. Bronze trophies are lowered. Masks of barbarous gods appear to a clamour of drums, sticks, the chant of a tribal triumph. A procession of warriors, chiefs and the wives of MAKAK in splendid tribal costumes gather, chanting to drums.

CHORUS
These are the conquests of Makak,
King of Limpopo, eye of Zambezi, blazing spear.

WARRIORS
Aieeee!

CHORUS
Who has bundled the tribes like broken sticks,
Masai, Zulu, Ibo, Coromanti,
Who has scattered his enemies like grain in the wind.

WARRIORS
Aieeee!

CHORUS
Drinkers of milk from the Mountains of the Moon.

Who has held captivity captive,
Who has bridled the wind,
Who has fathered the brood of the crocodile.
Whose eye is the sun,
Whose plate is the moon at its full,
Whose sword is the moon in its crescent.
Praise him!

WARRIORS
[*Chanting in antiphon*] Aieeee!

CHORUS
And we are his wives
For whom the sea knits its wool,
Robes without seam
Who is brother to God.

[*The volume increases*]

WARRIORS
Aieee!

CHORUS
Drinker of rivers,
In whom Gods waken,
Die, are reborn.

WARRIORS
[*Leaping in the air*] Aieeee!

CHORUS
Borne by the hands of the four corners of the earth on his
golden stool.

[MAKAK, *carried on a magnificent litter, enters. A golden stool is set down. The* CORPORAL, *also garbed magnificently in tribal robes, enters, with* SOURIS *some distance behind*]

CORPORAL

[*Softly*]

He whose peace is the counsel of the sea, gentler than cotton.

CHORUS

Whose hands are washed continually in milk,
Whose voice is the dove,
Whose eye is the cloud.

CORPORAL

Who shall do unto others as to him it was done.
Behold too, Basil, a dark ambassador,
Behold Pamphilion, apotheosised.

CHORUS

Who drew the thief to his bosom,
The murderer to his heart,
Whose blackness is a coal,
Whose soul is a fire,
Whose mind is a diamond,
Dispenser of justice,
Genderer and nourisher to a thousand wives,
Praise him!

[*All have assembled. The* CORPORAL *steps forward, then addresses* MAKAK]

CORPORAL

Inventor of history! [*Kisses* MAKAK'S *foot*]

MAKAK

I am only a shadow.

CORPORAL

Shh. Quiet, my prince.

MAKAK

A hollow God. A phantom.

CORPORAL

Wives, warriors, chieftains! The law takes no sides, it changes the complexion of things. History is without pardon, justice hawk-swift, but mercy everlasting. We have prisoners and traitors, and they must be judged swiftly. The law of a country is the law of that country. Roman law, my friends, is not tribal law. Tribal law, in conclusion, is not Roman law. Therefore, wherever we are, let us have justice. We have no time for patient reforms. Mindless as the hawk, impetuous as lions, as dried of compassion as the bowels of a jackal. Elsewhere, the swiftness of justice is barbarously slow, but our progress cannot stop to think. In a short while, the prisoners shall be summoned, so prepare them, Basil and Pamphilion. First, the accused, and after them, the tributes.

[*The prisoners are presented*]

Read them, Basil!

They are Noah, but not the son of Ham, Aristotle, I'm
skipping a bit, Abraham Lincoln, Alexander of Macedon,
Shakespeare, I can cite relevant texts, Plato, Copernicus,
Galileo and perhaps Ptolemy, Christopher Marlowe, Rob-
ert E. Lee, Sir John Hawkins, Sir Francis Drake, The
Phantom, Mandrake the Magician. [*The* TRIBES *are laughing*] It's not funny, my Lords, Tarzan, Dante, Sir Cecil
Rhodes, William Wilberforce, the unidentified author of
The Song of Solomon, Lorenzo de Medici, Florence Night-
ingale, Al Jolson, Horatio Nelson, and, but why go on?
Their crime, whatever their plea, whatever extenuation
of circumstances, whether of genius or geography, is, that
they are indubitably, with the possible exception of Alex-
andre Dumas, Sr. and Jr., and Alexis, I think it is Pushkin,
white. Some are dead and cannot speak for themselves, but
a drop of milk is enough to condemn them, to banish them
from the archives of the bo-leaf and the papyrus, from the
waxen tablet and the tribal stone. For you, my Lords, are
shapers of history. We wait your judgement, O tribes.

TRIBES

Hang them!

BASIL

It shall be done. The list continues *ad nauseam. [His voice
fades under a medley of screams and a drum roll of execu-
tion*] So much for the past. Consider the present. Petitions,
delegations, ambassadors, signatories, flatterers, potentates,
dominions and powers, sects, ideologies, special dispensa-

tions, wait politely on him fearing revenge. [*Reads from a ledger*] An offer to the Pope.

[MAKAK *shakes his head*]

TRIBES
No!

CORPORAL
Unanimous negative. [*He throws away the letter*]

BASIL
An invitation to be President of the United States?

[MAKAK *shakes his head*]

TRIBES
Impossible!

[CORPORAL *throws away the letter*]

CORPORAL
Unanimous negative.

BASIL
An apology in full from the Republic of South Africa.

[MAKAK *shakes his head, the pace increases*]

CORPORAL
Unanimous negative! [*Throws away the letter*]

BASIL
An offer to revise the origins of slavery. A floral tribute of lilies from the Ku Klux Klan. Congratulations from sev-

eral Golf and Country Clubs. A gilt-edged doctorate from the Mississippi University. The Nobel Peace Prize. One thousand dollars from a secret admirer. An autograph of Pushkin. The Stalin Peace Prize. An offer from the UN. A sliver of bone from the thigh of Lumumba. An offer from Hollywood. [*Throws all the letters away*]

TRIBES

No!

CORPORAL

Unanimous negative! Now, the prisoners.

[MOUSTIQUE, *bleeding and broken, is brought in*]

MOUSTIQUE

How am I guilty?

CORPORAL

You have betrayed our dream.

MOUSTIQUE

I am talking to you, Makak. [MAKAK *looks away*] Again, I must die, again?

CORPORAL

This is a lion. You are an insect whining in his ear.

MOUSTIQUE

Look around you, old man, and see who betray what. Is this what you wanted when you left Monkey Mountain? Power or love? Who are all these new friends? You can turn a blind eye on them, because now you need them.

314

But can you trust them for true? Oh, I remember you, in those days long ago, you had something there [*Touching his breast*], but here all that gone. All this blood, all this killing, all this revenge. So go ahead, kill me. Go ahead. Is for the cause? Go ahead then.

MAKAK

I will be different.

MOUSTIQUE

No, you will be no different. Every man is the same. Now you are really mad. Mad, old man, and blind. Once you loved the moon, now a night will come when, because it white, from your deep hatred you will want it destroyed.

MAKAK

My hatred is deep, black, quiet as velvet.

MOUSTIQUE

That is not your voice, you are more of an ape now, a puppet. Which lion? [*Sings: I don't know what to say this monkey won't do . . .*]

CORPORAL

You waste time, your Majesty. We have other cases, and justice must be done. Even tribal justice. What says the tribunal?

TRIBES

Next!

MAKAK

Take him away! [*Softly*] Moustique! Moustique!

CORPORAL

And now a pale, pathetic appeal for forgiveness.

[*The* APPARITION *is brought in*]

MAKAK

Who are you? Who are you? Why have you caused me all this pain? Why are you silent? Why did you choose me? O God, I was happy on Monkey Mountain.

CORPORAL

She, too, will have to die. Kill her, behead her, and you can sleep in peace.

MAKAK

The moon sinks in the sea and rises again, no sea can extinguish it. I will never rest. Tell me please, who are you? I must do what my people want.

CORPORAL

Bring me a blade, Souris. This is a job for a king, and, your Majesty, you cannot escape it. [SOURIS *brings him a curved sword.* CORPORAL *puts it in* MAKAK's *hand*] You will displease your wives, your sons, the vision is exhausted, her silence is enough.

MAKAK

Let the rest go. Leave us alone.

CORPORAL

You don't mind, I have to record this for history. For the people. If General Souris and I remain behind. I understand, I understand. It is a private matter. Out, wait outside. We will show you her head.

> [*All withdraw except* SOURIS, CORPORAL, BASIL, MAKAK *and the* WOMAN]

MAKAK

Is she there? Do you see her now?

CORPORAL

Of course. Don't you, General?

SOURIS

Plain as the moon.

CORPORAL

Time, time, your Majesty.

> [MAKAK *steps down and stands over the* WOMAN, *whose back is towards him*]

MAKAK

I remember.

CORPORAL

We have no time. We have no time.

MAKAK

Please. [*He looks at the moon, then he lifts the back of her hair*] I remember, one day, when I was younger, fifty years old, or so, I wake up, alone, and I do not know myself. I wake up, an old man that morning, with my clothes stinking of fifty years of sweat. My eye closing with gum, my two hands trembling, trembling when I open them, so, and I look in them, with all the marks like rivers, like a dead tree, and I ask myself, in a voice I do not know: Who you are, *negre?* I say to the voice and to my hands, with the black coal in the cuts, I say, your name is what—an old man without a mirror. And I went in the little rain barrel behind my hut and look down in the quiet, quiet water at my face, an old, cracked, burn-up face, with the hair turning white. And it was Makak. So I say, if you dead now, if you dead now. Well what? No woman will cry for you, no child will look at your face in death, as if it was the first time. The water in the rain barrel will show the cloud changing, and, as it have no memory, will forget your face. It will show the hawk passing smaller than a fly, and it will lick a dead leaf with its tongue, but you will go under this earth and burn and change as if you were a coal yourself, *charbonnier.* A big, big loneliness possess me, as if I was happy once, and strong, but could not remember where, as if, in some way, I was not no charcoal-burner, God be blessed, but a king, and I feel strongly to go down the mountain, and to reach the sea, as if the place I remember was across the sea. Before I do this thing, tell me who she is.

CORPORAL

She, she? What you beheld, my prince, was but an image of your longing. As inaccessible as snow, as fatal as leprosy. Nun, virgin, Venus, you must violate, humiliate, destroy her; otherwise, humility will infect you. You will come out in blotches, you will be what I was, neither one thing nor the other. Kill her! Kill her!

MAKAK

I cannot! I cannot!

CORPORAL

She is the wife of the devil, the white witch. She is the mirror of the moon that this ape look into and find himself unbearable. She is all that is pure, all that he cannot reach. You see her statues in white stone, and you turn your face away, mixed with abhorrence and lust, with destruction and desire. She is lime, snow, marble, moonlight, lilies, cloud, foam and bleaching cream, the mother of civilization, and the confounder of blackness. I too have longed for her. She is the colour of the law, religion, paper, art, and if you want peace, if you want to discover the beautiful depth of your blackness, nigger, chop off her head! When you do this, you will kill Venus, the Virgin, the Sleeping Beauty. She is the white light that paralysed your mind, that led you into this confusion. It is you who created her, so kill her! kill her! The law has spoken.

MAKAK

I must, I must do it alone.

CORPORAL

All right!

[SOURIS, CORPORAL *and* BASIL *withdraw*]

MAKAK

[*Removing his robe*] Now, O God, now I am free.

> [*He holds the curved sword in both hands and brings it down. The* WOMAN *is beheaded*]

BLACKOUT

Epilogue

The cell bars descend. TIGRE, SOURIS and MAKAK in jail.

MAKAK

Felix Hobain, Felix Hobain . . .

> [*The* CORPORAL *returns into the spotlight, holds up the mask*]

TIGRE

Mooma, don't cry,
You son in the jail a'ready
You son in the jail a'ready . . .

CORPORAL

What is your name?

MAKAK

Hobain . . . My name is Felix Hobain . . .

CORPORAL

I must itemise these objects. What is your race? What is or has been your denominational affiliation?

SOURIS

What he in for, Corporal?

MAKAK

My name is Felix Hobain . . . Hobain, I believe in my
God. I have never killed a fly. And I cannot sleep. Where
is General Tiger? Where is General Rat?

TIGRE

All night, with no sleep.

CORPORAL

Your name is Hobain. I must mark that on the charge.

MAKAK

Charge? What charge?

SOURIS

Drill him, Constable, drill him . . .

CORPORAL

Shut up! Charge? The reason why you in jail. It is only for
a night, and the moon is growing thin. When the sun rises,
I will let you go. You live up there? on Monkey Mountain?

MAKAK

Yes. *Oui*. Hobain. Sur Morne Macaque, *charbonnier*. I
does burn and sell coals. And my friend . . . well, he is
dead . . . Sixty-five years I have. And they calling me
Makak, for my face, you see? Is as I so ugly.

322

TIGRE

Get a lawyer, old man, to fix your face.

CORPORAL

I see uglier than that already, friend.

MAKAK

Then why am I here? What happen to me?

CORPORAL

Drunk and disorderly. You break up the shop of Felicien Alcindor yesterday, Saturday, on market day. I watch you quarrelling, preaching in the market. You insulted a friend of mine, Market Inspector Caiphas J. Pamphilion. You called a poor carpenter an agent of death. Then you start drinking, and before you cause more damage, I bring you in here. You had a rough night, friend. But is a first offence. Now, what is this? [*Holds up the mask*] Everybody round here have one. Why you must keep it, cut it, talk to it?

TIGRE

You like white woman, eh, old man? I can imagine your dreams . . .

SOURIS

Look, look, look, I see it. The face of the sun moving over the floor. Is morning . . .

CORPORAL

Niggers, cannibals, savages! Stop turning this place into a

stinking zoo. Believe me, old man [*Unlocking the cell*], it
have no salvation for them, and no hope for us. [MAKAK
steps out] You want this? [MAKAK *looks at the mask*]

MAKAK

And what day is this?

CORPORAL

It is market Saturday, it was, when you came. It is Sunday
morning now. [*Singing can be heard*] That noise is from
the Church of Revelation. You want this?

[MAKAK *shakes his head*]

SOURIS

Go with God, old man.

TIGRE

What happen, nigger, you going soft in your old age?

CORPORAL

Go on. Go home. There, Monkey Mountain. Walk through
the quiet village. I will explain everything to Alcindor.
Sometimes, there is so much pressure . . . Go on. You are
free. It is your first offence.

MAKAK

Moustique . . . There was a man called Moustique.

CORPORAL

Listen to them, listen to the sisters. All night. Well, some
find it in rum, some find it in religion.

[*A voice outside: "Corporal! Corporal!"*]

MOUSTIQUE

[*Entering with crocus bags*] You have a man here named Felix Hobain. They calling him Mak . . .

MAKAK

Is you? Is you, Moustique?

MOUSTIQUE

Time and tide wait for no man. What happen to you? What he do, Corporal? You must forgive him. He live alone too long, and he does catch fits. When the full moon come, a frenzy does take him. Ah, Felix Hobain, poor old Felix Hobain. Since yesterday morning I looking for you. I went up the Mountain, you wasn't at home. And you know Alcindor promise us two bags? What happen? I hear how you mash up Alcindor café . . . I have Berthilia outside . . . If is any damage, Corporal, I will pay you for it. Sometimes, in life, Corporal, a man can take no more . . . He don't know why he born, why he suffer, and that is what happen . . .

CORPORAL

He had a fit here. I thought he was drunk. A night in jail, I thought, would fix him.

MOUSTIQUE

He is a good man, Corporal. Let me take him where he belong. He belong right here.

CORPORAL

Here is a prison. Our life is a prison. Look, is the sun.

TIGRE

My breakfast, Lestrade. I want my damn breakfast. And I want blood. Meat, you understand?

SOURIS

Walk with God, grandfather. Walk with God.

MAKAK

[*Turning to them*] God bless you both. Lord, I have been washed from shore to shore, as a tree in the ocean. The branches of my fingers, the roots of my feet, could grip nothing, but now, God, they have found ground. Let me be swallowed up in mist again, and let me be forgotten, so that when the mist open, men can look up, at some small clearing with a hut, with a small signal of smoke, and say, "Makak lives there. Makak lives where he has always lived, in the dream of his people." Other men will come, other prophets will come, and they will be stoned, and mocked, and betrayed, but now this old hermit is going back home, back to the beginning, to the green beginning of this world. Come, Moustique, we going home.

CHORUS

I going home, I going home,
I going home, I going home,
I going home, I going home,
To me father's kingdom . . .

> [MAKAK *and* MOUSTIQUE *are walking back towards the* Mountain]

CURTAIN

326